Living by
HEART

A Guide to Discovering
Your Harmony Within

Living by Heart: A Guide to Discovering Your Harmony Within
2025 fEMPOWER Press Trade Paperback Edition
Copyright © 2025 Heather M. Haigh

Published in Canada, for Global Distribution by fEMPOWER Publications
www.fempower.pub
For more information email: media@fempower.pub

ISBN trade paperback: 978-1-998721-06-1
eBook: 978-1-998721-07-8

To order additional copies of this book: media@fempower.pub

Living by HEART

A Guide to Discovering Your Harmony Within

HEATHER M. HAIGH

Table of Contents

Author's REFLECTION

WHY WRITE THIS BOOK?

Have you ever received a message from the universe? The message could come directly, like a voice speaking to you, or it could come as an instinct, something pulling you toward an action. Perhaps you received a message to pick up this book at this very moment. You aren't quite sure why, but something tells you it's time.

The universe sent me a message recently.

It is time.
Time for what?
It is time to write.
Is it?
Yes.

Well, it's about time!

You see, I've always loved writing. I don't remember a time when I didn't love it. Whether journaling, writing poetry (especially in my teenage "angst" years), fiction, or work articles, writing has been an outlet for me my whole life.

But writing this book feels scary. It feels like pressure—to sit down and write about what is alive and bursting from within me on paper and share it with you in this way.

Do you recognize the fear I'm talking about? The fear that prevents you from taking that job opportunity that feels risky yet excites you? The fear that prevents you from asking for a promotion, asking for what you want in your relationship, or setting boundaries for yourself? The fear that stops you from action? Isn't it amazing how our minds create stories that keep us stuck?

As if writing this book were somehow different from writing on Facebook or LinkedIn.

I've been sharing parts of this story, excerpts of it, for more than twelve years now. By the time this book is in your hands, it will be thirteen years.

Perhaps that's what makes writing it now scary. The fact that I've been on this journey for thirteen years. I've come so far, and yet from here, in this moment, I feel like I am starting over. That feels so incredibly frustrating. *Oh, hello, Judger self.*

My heart sighs and smiles.

Yes, I expect as I share it with you, I'll have many visits from all my parts. My judger self will pop in often to criticize me. She's worried I am being too vulnerable and wants to protect me. *I love you, Judger self.*

My action self is the one insisting I sit down and write.

I am honoring you too, Action self. Thank you for kicking my ass.

My heart, the central focus for this book, she's the one who offers a gentle nod of encouragement. She's the one that I hear whisper *yes* when I am unsure whether it is safe to step forward. She's the voice I hear when I ask, "How can I get through this?" She answers, *Gently.*

It might seem strange to hear me talk about myself in terms of parts. When I was younger, I didn't have language for it. But I always sensed that the different thoughts in my head weren't connected to each other.

In working with my coaching clients, I found that they also experienced hearing many different messages in their heads, thoughts that often seemed disconnected or in conflict with each other. Can you relate?

Knowing that my clients and I all experienced these conflicting messages made me exceedingly curious about whether we indeed had different parts within ourselves.

When I studied to become a professional coach in 2016, I learned about my inner critic and inner ally. Through this initial work, I discovered that I had more than one critical voice in my head. My coaching instructor called it my "Itty Bitty Sh*tty Committee." I loved that name so much, it stuck.

I got to know my multiple inner critics as my "warrior self" who loved to battle and win, my "judger self" who loved to criticize everything, my "comparison self" who constantly compared me to others, my "diva self" who evaluated my worthiness on stage and in social situations, and my "librarian self" who was my inner taskmaster that focused on getting sh*t done, no matter what. I desperately tried to silence my "committee" and struggled to live peacefully with all those voices.

I also came to know my inner allies: my "heart" who helped me see the world and myself through the eyes of love, and my "higher self" who connected me with the universe.

In 2022 I discovered the Internal Family Systems (IFS) framework that believes all your parts matter and all your parts are worthy of love. All parts were created with the intention to take care of you.

Years before IFS crossed my path, I was building a vision for "whole-self living" with the belief that we're not supposed to be guided solely from our heads. We're meant to be guided by our hearts too, as well as our bodies, our guts, our souls. We're meant to listen to all parts of ourselves—each part holding its own wisdom.

The challenge was that IFS was created for psychologists and therapists, and I was a coach. In 2023 a coaching friend referred me to a Parts Work for Coaches program where I learned how to use parts work for myself and with my clients, and to understand the clear distinction between therapy and coaching in this work.

For me, doing this inner work helped me end a battle between my heart and my warrior self that raged within me for more than forty years. Parts Work confirmed something I'd always struggled with: I didn't need to rid myself of parts—not even the Itty Bitty Sh*tty Committee. I could become an integrated "whole" person instead, by accepting and loving all my parts: a compassionate warrior.

As a coach and whole-self advocate, I could coach my clients with Parts Work and invite them to explore their whole-self connecting with and loving all their parts.

Before I started this journey, I had no idea how "out of tune" I was with my parts, especially my heart.

As you read this book, I invite you to notice the different parts of yourself. Perhaps your judger self is judging whether you really want to connect with all your parts. Or perhaps your judger self is judging me and whether this is really the book for you. The judger self often shows up to protect you. Perhaps it's worried that this book may ask you to connect with your heart, with your emotions. To get vulnerable. *Hello, Judger self! Welcome to the party.*

HOW DID WE DISCONNECT FROM OUR HEARTS?

We were born with strong connections to our hearts. Our hearts communicate the emotions within us, and from birth, those emotions have been flowing through us without attachment or meaning. But over time, we began receiving messages that taught us to control, manage, or even stop our emotions:

"Don't cry!"
"Stop yelling!"
"Suck it up!"

By the time we reach adulthood, we've created stories and barriers that prevent us from connecting with our hearts and our emotions. New messages are added, such as "Don't be so emotional," "Never let them see you cry," and "Emotions make you look weak." Then there's my personal favorite: "Put on your big girl panties and get on with it."

It's no wonder we've stopped connecting with our hearts! How could we possibly be successful if we showed any emotions in the workplace? I've encountered too many women crying in bathroom stalls at the office. I was one of them.

We've spent years working hard to control, manage, suppress, or eliminate our emotions entirely. We've spent years reinforcing beliefs that we need to think with our heads, use facts and evidence to prove our thinking, to be "practical."

In fact, you may be thinking:

If I live by heart, I won't be rational.
If I live by heart, I'll look weak.
If I let my emotions in, I won't be able to regain control.

Living by heart is about releasing the myth that rational, fact-based, logical thinking is the only way to live. Our hearts were designed to support us, inform us, and guide us. Our hearts tell us vital information—if only we listen.

The effort it takes us to "manage" our emotions drains us. When we judge our emotions, we also work hard to try to control them. Might they be controlling us more than we think?

When we remove judgment and let our emotions flow through us, without force, there is nothing to control. It just is. That's where freedom lives. When we ask what our emotions are meant to tell us, we connect with the messages intended to guide our choices. When we hide our emotions out of fear of appearing weak or trying to "be strong," we can come across as cold, impersonal, unfeeling, or emotionless.

Our authentic selves are inextricably linked to our hearts. It's our vulnerability and willingness to use our emotions as superpowers that show true strength. And courage. Our vulnerability connects us with the world. It's what makes us relatable and likable. Our hearts are where humanity lies.

I've learned so much on my living by heart journey that I want to share with you.

While I've always been a warrior, I'm also an emotional person. I cry a lot. I cry when I'm happy, sad, even when I'm angry—especially when I'm angry! Before I started living by heart, I believed my emotions were bad and signs of weakness. I constantly apologized when my emotions got the better of me.

"I'm sorry to be so emotional."
"I don't mean to cry, but . . ."
"Sorry for being an emotional mush ball."

I remember one specific situation when I was so angry and discouraged. I needed to speak to my boss and clearly represent myself. Instead, I cried with rage. My tears distracted from the matter at hand, and I spent the whole time apologizing for crying instead of embracing my emotions as my superpowers and standing up for myself.

Today, I know I'd use that emotion completely differently. I'd embrace my tears, let my boss know they reflected how angry I felt, and communicate what I needed from him. No apology required.

If you're wondering how I made such a dramatic shift, it didn't happen overnight.

I learned to have compassion for my emotions, instead of judgment. I learned to observe my emotions as information, receive the messages from my heart openly, and see the wisdom my heart knows. When I did that, I started to feel more balanced, more honest, more authentic, and more courageous.

I wish I could tell you that living by heart is easy. Or even that it came easily to me. I wish I could tell you that in this book I'll give you "Three Easy Steps" to do it. This isn't that book, but there are steps you can take to live by your heart that I share along with stories from my own journey.

On my journey to living by heart, I had painful moments— moments when I would be so mad at myself.

What the hell is wrong with me?
I know better than this.
This shouldn't be so hard.

The angrier I was at myself, the harder my journey got, the more impossible it felt, and the more certain I became that I would never feel that calm ease I craved. I mistakenly assumed that because I'd done all the work, I should be at the destination. But living by heart is a daily practice, not a destination.

Understanding my parts—especially the critical committee creating all the noise in my head—and building a practice to listen to them and connect with my heart helped me navigate back to center, back into harmony with my parts.

You can expect that you'll experience some judgment, impatience, frustration, and maybe even some anger along the way. It's all part of the process. You'll also build a practice that can support you to live in harmony with your parts, as your authentic self. As a compassionate warrior.

INTRODUCTION

Growth and the Journey Inward

Have you ever felt like you're running on a treadmill and can't get off? Have you ever looked at your life and thought, *I'm checking all the boxes. Why does it feel like something is still missing?* Have you ever thought, *I want to feel like I'm enough?*

These are just a few of the thoughts I had before I started my journey to living by heart. If you have thoughts like these running through your head today, know that you're not alone. As a professional coach, I see many people struggling to get off this veritable treadmill, to find greater meaning in their lives; I've seen many people holding a deep desire to believe they are more than enough.

I traveled solo when I started my journey to living by heart, but I'm here to take you on this journey with me as you learn to live by heart as well. As you take the steps, I'll share some of the experiences I've had along the way to remind you that you aren't alone, to encourage you, and to even give you a chuckle or two. While some of the stories I tell you might bring up unexpected responses, others will help you find your way out of discomfort into empathy, and perhaps even humor. Laughter, even at ourselves, can bring lightness when the work feels a little heavy.

If laughing at yourself feels harsh, it may be your "judger self" having the giggles. Together, we'll work on laughing at ourselves from our hearts—with kindness and lightness—which lets us take ourselves a bit less seriously.

I can say with certainty that if you're willing to look inward, if you're willing to do the work, if you're willing to get a little uncomfortable (because, let's face it, looking inward can get somewhat uncomfortable), and if you're willing to try doing things differently, you will see change.

What keeps you stuck is both **fear** and **comfort**.

Fear? I'm not afraid of anything.

If this was your reaction to what I just said, then I understand. We can come back to fear in a bit and start with comfort now.

When it comes to comfort, it's easy to default to old habits and patterns. Sticking with what you know and with what comes easily may feel effortless, but it can also make you feel helpless. Staying in the comfort zone feeds the feelings of "not enough." When you don't take on new challenges or invest in your own growth, your inner critic jumps for joy because your fear of failure, of being inadequate, has just been confirmed: *See, I told you that you couldn't do it.*

We know intuitively, though, that there's no growth in the comfort zone. So, if you choose to start living by heart, you'll grow. But you need to be prepared to experience discomfort.

Is there any good news? you may be wondering. Yes, there's good news!

Think about the journey to living by heart like learning how to swim. While there will be some discomfort, you choose how fast you learn and where you want to start. You can choose to dive into the deep end, or you can wade slowly into shallow waters, testing the temperature first. You can choose to go at your own pace. In fact, you can choose to stop and start at any time. I've stopped and started, fallen, and gotten up to start again countless times. Living by heart isn't an event, it's a lifelong adventure! The discomfort is temporary, and the benefits last a lifetime.

Now, let's return to the feeling of fear. The word "fear" creates fear, doesn't it?

It also creates resistance.

I don't want to feel fear.
Fear feels hard.

I'd rather do things that feel good/safe/certain.

I understand that instinct well. I also know that fear and comfort love each other. Fear is what drives you back to comfort. Fear lives in between comfort and growth because the discomfort is what makes you afraid, and so even before you have time to get uncomfortable, fear stops you and pulls you back to comfort—to safety.

What if you could stop running? What if you redefined the boxes you'd focused on ticking off and found the meaning you've been looking for outside of predetermined checklists? What if you already *knew*, in your bones, that you're more than enough but are afraid to admit it to yourself? Would it be worth it to step into fear and discomfort, knowing that something great is on the other side?

Before you answer, take a moment to consult your heart. Place one or both hands on your heart, take a breath or two, close your eyes, and ask yourself: "What does my heart want?"

If your heart tells you to go for it, then let's get started.

What Is Living by Heart?

To understand what living by heart is, let's start by looking at what it isn't.

Our North American society tends to overvalue thinking and undervalue feeling. Expressions like "facts over feelings," "don't be emotional," and "look for the evidence," reinforce the idea that intellect is the only capital that matters. As a result, despite being born with both thoughts and feelings that guide us, we've become overly dependent on our minds and sadly disconnected from our hearts.

Living by heart doesn't mean abandoning your thoughts, your knowledge, or the wisdom you've gained from years of experience. It doesn't mean you turn on the emotional floodgates and weep or rage all the time, or that you're dominated by your emotions and aren't responsible for your own self-management. Quite the contrary.

Living by heart is about inviting your heart to join the conversation. It means that you listen to your heart as deeply as you're already listening to your head.

It sounds so simple, yet it isn't easy.

There is unlearning that must happen along with the new learning. Fortunately, our brains are agile and capable of adapting to changes in how we connect with our thoughts and feelings.

The study of neuroplasticity helps explain why it's so much easier for you to do what you've always done. The neural pathways in the brain have been established through your habits and routines, so the mind follows those pathways. To create new neural pathways, you need to get out of your comfort zone. The steps in this book are designed to help you challenge your thinking, get outside that comfort zone, and create new neural pathways.

Connecting with your heart takes work. It's an inward journey. After years of programming to prioritize thinking over feeling, learning to connect with your heart requires daily practice just like going to the gym or practicing yoga. To live by heart, you need to go to the heart mat and bring your whole self.

From Heart to HEART

Take a moment to reflect on the word "heart." You may wish to capture your thoughts on paper.

When you think about the word "heart," what comes to mind? How would you describe it? Do you think about the heart as a muscle beating in your chest? Or do you think of the heart as symbolic of an emotion, a feeling, or something bigger?

What came up for you when I asked these questions?

At first, the word "heart" had one simple meaning for me—love. I wanted to feel more love. I wanted to see myself, others, and the world through the eyes of love. Once I realized that, I saw a shift in how I was viewing everything, and that was it. I focused on one small shift in my mindset to change the way I experienced life: I made the conscious choice to see the world through the eyes of love every day.

The meaning of "heart" has evolved. The journey to living by heart is more than one thing, it's a daily practice that looks at many aspects of yourself, who you are, and how you want to "be" in the world.

Over time, the meaning of the word expanded for me, just like my own heart did. In this book, I share with you the expansion of living by heart and the practices I use to support me living wholeheartedly today.

HEART represents five core practices:

1. **H – Healing**
2. **E – Empathy**
3. **A – Awareness**
4. **R – Resilience**
5. **T – Trust**

Living by heart is about bringing your heart into everything you do, but it isn't about abandoning the wisdom and experiences of your head or the habits of your body. It's about syncing all parts of yourself and finding harmony within. It means inviting the heart to lead at times, while at other times, you'll just tune into the heart momentarily to listen to what it offers you.

In **Healing**, you'll look inward to see if there's anything getting in the way of your connection with your heart. When I looked inward, I started uncovering the pain my warrior was concealing.

We each carry moments from our past that influence how we operate in the world today. Your journey inward is your own and likely quite different from mine. This work is critical to free your heart so you can openly give and receive.

In **Empathy**, the focus shifts outward. How are you impacting others around you? I share some moments that changed the way I see others and started to embody empathy. We'll look at how to develop more empathy, what embodying empathy looks like, and how you can choose to engage with people with love and compassion.

In **Awareness**, you'll look at your ego, your inner critic (or committee), and how the inner voices influence you. I discovered I have a whole inner critic committee! I'll share a few awareness experiences and how my own thinking hijacked me again and again. You'll gain insight into the way you experience situations and how you tend to respond. Through awareness, you shine a light on the shadows, giving you an opportunity to see yourself and start making choices from your heart. I found that after healing, the awareness work had the greatest impact on who I am today, and I'm excited to share how this work can impact you too.

In **Resilience**, the heart and body work together to maintain equilibrium and reduce stress. On my journey, I found that if I didn't fuel myself and access my resilience, it didn't matter how much awareness or empathy I had. I couldn't be my best self. Sometimes, when you focus on the inner work, it can be easy to forget that you need to refuel. In a world where terms like "overwhelm" and "burnout" are commonplace, you'll discover where your own resilience comes from and how you can tap into your incredible tank of resilience.

In **Trust**, you'll explore the barriers to trust and how learning to trust yourself can set you free. There is so much uncertainty in the world. It's constantly in a state of change, and there is little we truly control. Trust is vital to help you live and lead by heart. I talk about the various types of trust, share a few lessons I learned, and describe the three types of trust I practice every day.

The following image visualizes how the five core practices of Living by HEART are intertwined, just like your journey to living by heart will intertwine the practices you learn along the way.

The five core practices don't have to happen independently or in a specific order. In fact, in my daily HEART work, I shift across all five practices depending on what I am feeling or experiencing, and where I assess I need to focus my attention. I do the same when I'm coaching my clients. Wherever they are in the moment is where we spend our time exploring. The book follows my own journey through the five core practices as I experienced them initially and then built them into the Living by HEART practice.

You may have strengths in different areas than I had at the start of my journey, and certain core practices may be where your deeper work lies. Come to this book with an open heart and an open mind. Be kind to yourself on the journey. Wherever you're starting from is exactly where you're supposed to be right now.

In the final section of the book, The Compassionate Warrior, I'll share the questions I ask myself to assess which of the five core practices needs more love and focus.

So, let's dive in.

I Need Some Heart

When you're repeatedly rewarded for being strong, confident, and dominant, you believe it's the best way to be. When you watch others who are strong, confident, and dominant get rewarded as well, it confirms that belief. You may even form a bias.

Perhaps you've been told you have a "strong personality." If you have strong opinions, a strong voice, and a strong sense of self, you may be a warrior, like me.

I was born a warrior, and throughout my life, my warrior kept getting validated. As a child, my warrior side was rewarded in verbal battles with my sister, intellectual debates with my corporate lawyer dad, and through numerous leadership roles at school, extracurricular activities, and summer camp.

As a teenager, my warrior self negotiated with my teachers, battled with my parents, and challenged authority wherever I encountered it. The reward was positive reinforcement from my friends. I was seen as a risk-taker, which was courageous and cool.

When I entered the workforce, my warrior side grew stronger. She fought for me to pursue opportunities that scared me. She questioned processes and policies, advocated for change, and demanded opportunities for growth and challenge. The more I showed my warrior side, the more I was rewarded.

I also started receiving feedback that I intimidated other people, especially women. *Ouch.* Hearing that feedback brought on a flood of emotions. First, it really hurt. I felt sharp, stabbing pain and wanted to cry, but I didn't let myself stay in that feeling for long. Second, I felt angry and defensive. *Oh, hello, Warrior.*

Were men getting this kind of feedback? Or was it a gender bias stating that women can't be confident, strong, and courageous without making other women feel weak?

Thinking about it that way strengthened my warrior. She would fight harder. *Just watch me!*

For a long time, I had an insatiable need to win. My warrior tended to dominate the other parts of myself, especially my heart—the loving, nurturing part of me that craved connection. Today, I see something I couldn't see then.

My first feeling, the hurt and wanting to cry, was my heart trying to get my attention. I was so used to leaning into my warrior, I didn't realize that I ignored my heart. I pushed her away. I thought my warrior was my heart in action.

What was my warrior? Ego. She was ego all wrapped up with fear.

Years of conditioning and years of rewarding my warrior had caused me to place my heart in the deepest, darkest recesses of my soul. When she tried to get my attention, I quickly dismissed her with a "No, thank you!"

I didn't realize that my heart was a vital part of feeling whole. I didn't realize that with my heart, I didn't have to fight so hard for everything. I didn't know that living by heart could make my life easier.

Doing the Inner Work

Doing the inner work takes time. You need to get to know all the "parts" of yourself. The loud and dominant parts, the softer and quieter parts, and even the silent parts that have been muted for some time. You may be familiar with certain parts; others you might meet for the first time. If you've already done some of this work, you'll know your inner critic and perhaps your inner ally too. If you're just getting started, not to worry. This book will help you identify the parts of yourself and get to know them better.

When it comes to my inner dialogue, where my heart and my warrior self meet, one wants peace and the other wants to fight. My heart invites possibility and my warrior self cries out: *War!*

My heart responds: *Okay, love. Go that way if you want.*

Then my judger self chimes in: *Stop being so agreeable! What's wrong with you?!*

Sometimes it can get a little noisy and crowded in my head. My warrior self and judger self are part of what my coaching instructor called my "Itty Bitty Sh*tty Committee." In this book, let's call them the IBSC for short.

Sometimes my warrior self likes to invite the IBSC over for drinks. Her favorite IBSC pals are Comparison self and Judger self. While Comparison self and Judger self are twins, they're fraternal and prefer not to be confused for each other. Especially my Comparison self! Call her "Judger" and she will just lose it.

So, what does the IBSC have to do with awareness and living by heart? You need to meet, manage, and have conversations with the parts of yourself, especially the parts that love to get in your way. Whether you have one solo inner critic or an entire committee, living by heart is about living as your whole authentic self.

When I first started my journey inward, I got excited. I was learning so much about myself, and I was feeling transformed by it. A few people in the early days told me, "It's just the age you've entered." That bugged me. It's as if you suddenly gain insights you didn't have the day before when you were "younger." It's dismissive and invalidates your lived experience.

Through my inner work, I now choose to believe that when I receive a statement that sounds dismissive, it's accidental. Choosing that perspective helps me manage my potential anger and reaction to that person.

I don't believe this work "comes with age." I've seen many "older" people who don't have the "wisdom" some people dismissively assume "comes with age." I've also met many "young" people with significantly greater insight, self-awareness, and wholeness than their elders. It's not about age.

Sometimes I let the voices of others in, and I feel paralyzed. I start questioning my own knowledge, experience, and worthiness. Does that ever happen to you when you are accidentally invalidated? Maybe you, too, experience the resulting downward spiral of thinking. *Is living by heart really a thing? Or is it just something everyone discovers as they get to a certain age?*

While you may care less about what other people think of you as you get older, and you may become more discerning, or more forgiving, living by heart is a practice. It doesn't just happen. You choose to consciously take a different path than the one society tells you a person "should" take.

Living by heart requires you to look deeply inward so you can see beyond yourself. That sounds strange. *How can looking inward help me see beyond myself better?*

Maybe this is a better way to look at it: What happens when you don't do the inner work first? Consider for a moment a pair of reflective sunglasses, the kind where you can see out, but others can't see your eyes behind the lenses. All they see is their own reflection.

When you wear reflective sunglasses, people can't really connect with you. Your eyes are veiled by the glass, thus creating a distance between you and others. A separation.

If I can't see your eyes, I can't tell if you're looking at me. I can't tell if you're feeling empathy, seeing my body language and expressions, or whether you even care about what I'm saying. The sunglasses are a mask that protects you and keeps me out.

One of my mentors used to say, "Trust cannot be built where judgment is present." Without the necessary information from your eyes, I feel judged.

When you haven't done the inner work, you may be walking around with reflective sunglasses, protecting yourself from the dangers of showing your authentic self to others. Exposure may feel too risky. You may feel that being vulnerable puts you at a disadvantage.

Now, consider you're wearing rose-colored glasses. I can see your eyes and perhaps even feel like I can trust you. However, you bring only your perception to the conversation. Everything is painted with a rosy tinge, from your experiences, biases, beliefs, and more. I may not know the lens through which you are looking, but you are overlaying every word you hear with your own assumptions and meaning making.

Rose-colored glasses might be less protective than reflective ones, but with rose-colored glasses on you can't really see what other people are experiencing. You can't be truly present, open, and curious when your colored lens is painted on top of everything you are taking in.

When you haven't done the inner work, you can't see the color of the lens you're bringing to the world. You hold tightly to the belief that you see the world how it is, and that your view is the right one. You may be wearing any color of glass lens—it doesn't have to be rose-colored. Whether blue, green, gray, orange, yellow, or brown, the color of your lens changes the way you experience the world.

When you do the inner work, you come to the world with clear glass that lets you observe what is, without judgment. Clear glass lets you be present, open, and curious. When you are present, open, and curious, you can be accepting and compassionate.

So, what is the inner work?

When I started doing my own inner work, I thought, *How hard can it really be?* I considered myself an evolved person who had spent years in my youth analyzing the world and myself in it. I thought I was light-years ahead of the game. But I was only scratching the surface, so to speak.

If the work seems easy when you start, you're likely doing what I call "surface inner work."

What? There are levels?

Yes, my love.

There are levels of inner work. And when you start doing the deeper inner work, you realize you've built stories at the surface to protect yourself, and some of those stories may not be serving you. You also uncover the parts of yourself, like your inner critic and IBSC (if you have a whole committee), who love to get in your way.

You can't just jump into the deeper inner work. You'll need to start at the surface before you can reach more depth.

Let's begin with a few assumptions:

1. We are complex beings made up of layers built by our experiences, values, beliefs, education, culture, religion, and so much more.
2. We all have various parts of ourselves. As Richard Schwartz, creator of Internal Family Systems (IFS), notes in his work, all parts matter, and all parts are worthy of love.
3. When we understand ourselves, we can better understand the systems we are a part of, others in those systems, and the world.

So, how do I do the deeper inner work?

You'll discover how to best connect with yourself as you read this book. There are many options. For example, some people meditate, some reflect while walking in nature, and some people journal.

I have found (as have many of my clients) that journaling can be an effective way to achieve a deeper understanding of ourselves. In this book you'll find journal prompts at the end of the sections as one option you can use to support your own inner work. You'll also find other tips and suggestions for building your own Living by HEART practice.

It's the "what" that is difficult to explain. The best word I've found to describe the inner work so far is "unraveling." Think of a rogue thread in the armpit of your sweater. When you find it, you think, *I'll just quickly pull that thread so it doesn't look like I am growing armpit hair.*

You grab the thread with the best of intentions and pull. Suddenly that beloved sweater has a hole in the armpit. *Damn. I loved that sweater. I wonder if I could stitch it back together.*

It's no use. As you try to fix the hole, the sweater unravels further.

The inner work and the stories you've built to protect you unravel just like the sweater. The more you pull on the thread, the more you uncover, learn, process—and the unraveling continues.

Don't worry about getting a hole in your sweater. This unraveling frees you from the limiting beliefs that have kept you stuck. Even though that sweater is comfortable, it's been holding you back from living authentically as your whole self with all your parts working harmoniously together. You won't need that sweater when you're living by heart. In fact, you may be surprised you held on to that sweater for so long.

I'll share in the section "The Healing Begins" that when I started this journey, I didn't intend to change anything other than my diet. I believed I was very self-aware and knew why I acted the way I did. I could admit my flaws and hold myself accountable, and I held everyone else accountable too. I was very comfortable in my sweater.

My certainty about myself and who I was in the world was what I extended to others. I believed I could "read" people, and I knew their intentions. I was an expert judger. I was also a perfectionist and a control freak. I expected everyone else to operate in the same way I did. If they didn't, I judged them. They weren't as dedicated. They weren't as driven. They weren't as capable. My sweater was better than their sweaters.

"They weren't, they weren't, they weren't . . ."

Hmm. I see a pattern here.

Yes, I lived in judgment of myself and others. All. The. Time. I just couldn't see it. It was like I got my sweater stuck over my head!

We'll talk more about judgment in this book. I've found, both in coaching and in workshops, that when I first talk about judgment, most people react with "Oh, I'm not judgmental like that" or "I don't judge other people."

If you're having a similar response, it is totally normal, and it's your "judger" judging the topic of judgment because it's uncomfortable. It's uncomfortable digging into your own judgment of yourself and of others—and doing so often causes more self-judgment. It may feel more comfortable keeping the sweater on.

When I was a corporate trainer, we used this quote to help teach new advisers how to build trust with their clients: "Trust cannot be built where judgment is present."

Yet, even as a trainer teaching others about trust and judgment, I couldn't see how my own judgment was preventing me from trusting myself and others. I said the words, but I didn't live them.

I had to dig deeper into my own inner work to first acknowledge my judgment, learn to accept it, then finally discover ways to skillfully manage it. Judgment is just one piece of the journey. There's so much more, and I'm so happy to share it with you.

What will the inner work unravel? I don't know what you'll discover about yourself along the journey. Like a custom-knitted sweater, you've lived a unique life, and you'll unravel unique moments, joys, and challenges. You'll need to choose what you want to do with them.

What I can tell you is that you'll likely identify some stories you've been carrying, stories that at one time served you but you may no longer need. You'll likely also uncover other stories that perhaps never really served you, and you can decide if you want to keep them, rewrite them, or let them go.

For example, when I committed to healing my body through diet and exercise after years of nutritional assault, some old stories I'd built about my body were suddenly challenged.

"I get sick all the time." After years of getting bronchitis three or four times a year, I stopped getting sick.

"I'm not a good sleeper." After years of staying up until one or two in the morning, I started sleeping well. I fell asleep easily at night and got eight straight hours.

"My stomach always gets upset." It stopped getting upset. In fact, so many of the stomach-related issues I had disappeared completely in a matter of weeks.

These "truths" I had been carrying for decades were shattered. I wondered what other "truths" about myself might not, in fact, be true. That curiosity opened other areas of my life to explore, areas to bust long-standing stories I'd built up over time, areas to create new ways of being.

That's why the inner work matters so much. It's about how you unravel your stories.

It's about connecting with the inner guidance of your heart to support you on the journey of unraveling. It's about looking deeply inward and finding love for yourself. It's about compassion and kindness. It's about getting off the treadmill, putting down the sword, stripping off the armor, and laying your heart and soul bare—in their worthiness.

It's about you living by heart.

The Heart Moves Forward, Not Back

As humans, we tend to want to go back to a moment or period when we felt good, or maybe better than we are feeling right now. Our minds filter out any negative aspects of this cherished past so that it appears idyllic.

We dream about returning there. Trying to get "there" again. Trying to feel "that way" again. What we fail to realize is that we have changed since that time. We are no longer those people. We can't go back, no matter how fiercely we try. Instead, we must journey forward and write a new story.

Living by heart isn't a journey "back" to something. It is a journey forward to something new. Something unknown that you can't see yet. Something yet to be defined. There is positive energy in it. There is possibility.

As I share the steps for Living by HEART with you, I'm also redefining what it means to me along the way. We're working on our individual journeys together.

I'm quite aware that the work I am doing will start creating a new way of living by heart. It is constantly evolving as I grow and change. I know where I am now and the intention of where I wish to get to, even though that new image of myself is not clear at present. That's the beautiful part—setting an intention, even if the outcome isn't clear.

Give yourself permission to see as far as you can see from here, knowing that down the road you'll be able to see further. Get excited about the journey ahead. Get excited about the learning along the way. Get excited about the possibilities that may emerge.

Ask yourself, "What will support me on this journey?"

You could consider: "What might help me stay grounded and focused?"

You could ask: "What will keep me in a loving, compassionate frame of mind?"

Here are a few thoughts I captured as I journaled about what I needed to support me in this next chapter of my living by heart journey. You may wish to use these as prompts for yourself or write your own.

- Listening to ambient music calms me and helps me focus. Music quickly connects me to my heart.
- Stretching and moving my body connects me to my heart.

Then, as I wrote about how showering in the morning helps me, my judger self showed up: *Who wants to read about that?*

It felt like a good time to invite my judger self to go outside and play for a while so I could continue exploring what might support me. But my judger self kept coming back and adding her less-than-helpful comments. Finally, my heart self (who I also call my higher self), with patience, curiosity, and compassion, invited my judger self to speak her mind.

And so began a Parts Work dialogue, right in the middle of my productive journaling session! My heart invited my productive self to go play on the swings so my heart and judger self could talk.

As they chatted, I realized that my productive self was judg-mental about my judger self. That made me laugh. I observed my authentic, higher self and my heart loving my judger self, listening to her and giving her room to share her truth and her fears. It was during this dialogue that I realized I was trying to "go back" to a past version of myself that no longer existed.

Something magical happens when you give all parts of yourself space and love so they can feel seen and valued: You start loving your whole self more. And loving yourself first is the foundation for living by heart. Throughout this book, I'll share a few of these inner dialogues with the different parts of myself, as they've re-ally helped me go deeper in understanding myself better and loving myself more.

When you love yourself deeply, you have more love to give others without feeling depleted. When you know yourself more, you trust yourself more.

I can tell you: I've been forever altered by events that have oc-curred over the past twelve years since I first began this love-led journey. The woman sitting here now writing this book is not the same woman who traveled a path to love-led living those many years ago.

If so much has changed, then what is the same? The inten-tion to love from the inside out and the knowledge that living by heart transforms the world around me—it is these that have been the constants for me. The insights I gained along the way from each challenge and opportunity where I led with love and saw the world shift before my eyes, felt the world move with my heart, are the insights I bring with me for the journey ahead.

This is what I want to share with you as you take the steps to your own heart in a whole new way. Today. With the woman you are now. Loving her, nurturing her, embracing her, and inviting her to dance like no one is watching. Walking with this incredible woman within you right now into an uncertain future that's filled with possibility.

There is a delightful ditty that I invite you to play, if music is part of your own journey, called "This Is the Beginning" by BOY. It's on my life's soundtrack, and I hear it playing right now as I embrace the journey forward, not back, to my heart. What's on your playlist?

HEALING

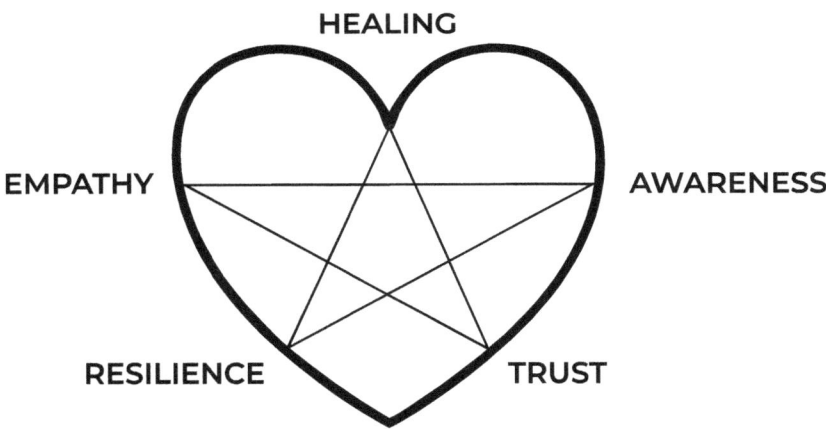

HEALING

EMPATHY   AWARENESS

RESILIENCE   TRUST

What Is Healing?

What comes to mind when you hear the word "healing"? Do you feel resistance or readiness? Do you notice your judger self stepping up with some opinions? I wouldn't be surprised if you do. I've always had a love/hate relationship with the word "healing."

I do believe we all need some form of healing—for our souls, hearts, and minds, as well as for our energetic and physical bodies. Each one of us has lived through experiences that shaped who we are today, and some of those experiences were challenging.

It's the idea of being some sort of "healer" that never really sat well with me. How does someone see themselves as a healer? I think part of my issue with the term and using it for myself relates to my own sense of worthiness. *Who am I to say that I am a healer?*

Then I hear my heart: *Who are you not to be?*

There are many wonderful professionals in the space of psychology, psychotherapy, and social work who are there for us when we need healing, or a healer's touch. The work of self-healing does not replace the invaluable work of professionals when it's appropriate for you or me to engage them.

In fact, I'm very comfortable with the idea of therapy. I've worked with different therapists over the course of my life: as a child when my parents separated, as a teenager when my pain was raw and exposed, and today as I navigate the grief of both parents passing within a few years of each other. I'm an advocate for getting the mental health support each of us needs.

So, when I talk about healing as a self-practice, I'm referring to the work each of us can do ourselves to better understand our thoughts and feelings, then work on what's getting in our own way. I believe that people are naturally "creative, resourceful, and whole," as I learned in my coaching training. You need to feel whole enough, safe enough, and supported enough to engage in your own healing work. You need to know yourself and your limits.

Note: If at any time you don't feel whole enough to do this work alone, it can be helpful to engage a professional to support you—this can be emotional work. Take care of yourself first and be kind to yourself. Go at your own pace.

I struggled with the question, "Am I a healer?" On one hand, I wanted to share what I was learning about my own healing with everyone, but to do that I thought I needed to be a healer. On the other hand, I didn't feel like I was enough.

So, after visiting a Reiki practitioner every week for a year and connecting with my whole self much more deeply, I decided to get my Reiki practitioner certification so I could begin to see myself as a healer rather than being the one needing the healing. I completed Levels 1 and 2, but even after that, I didn't really use Reiki on other people because I couldn't figure out how to talk about myself as a Reiki practitioner, a healer.

Twenty years of a corporate brain, plus all sorts of external messages that had been telling me the world believed that healing was "woo-woo," was a lot to unpack and shift. *I just need more training!* I thought.

When I completed a three-day immersive course to become a Tao Hands practitioner, I announced the news on Facebook. I was proud of the work I'd put in over those three days and proud that I was investing more in myself to bring greater service to the world.

My dad saw my post and called me. "What is a Tao Hand practitioner?" he asked, pronouncing Tao as T-ow instead of Dow. I hadn't expected anyone to ask me, so I wasn't prepared to answer him. I stumbled my way through a convoluted description, tripping on my words, repeating myself, and making it way more complicated than it needed to be.

My dad replied, "Oh, I am not interested in that at all."

Ouch. I felt an ache in my heart and the judgment washed over me.

I didn't tell him that I'd already invested in and completed Levels 1 and 2 of my Reiki practitioner certifications. I didn't tell him that I believed energy work was an important part of the coaching I did with my clients. I just sat with the ache in my heart from his words of disinterest.

See, my inner critic gleefully hissed, *you will never be accepted for this work. Why bother with it. What a waste of your time and money.*

I had a choice to make in that moment. I could accept that my dad's view was proof that my fear was real—that the truth was not what I believed but what the world believed—and accept that I'd wasted my time and money on "woo-woo" healing junk.

Or I could choose to believe my truth. I could choose to believe I'm here to serve and that this work is vital to healing ourselves, each other, the earth, and the universe. I could choose to believe that he simply wasn't ready to see that the world needs this work. He just wasn't ready *yet.*

I chose my truth.

I chose to embrace my purpose, my work, and my service to the world. I also chose to accept that not everyone I encountered wanted those services. And that's okay. I'd offer healing services to those who wanted to receive them, and I'd love and respect those who didn't, without taking their opinions so deeply into my own heart.

It felt so good to make that choice. And while my darling judger self tried to do her best to protect me from others' judgment and the potential pain of rejection, she seemed more resigned to my decision than usual.

I also answered the question I was struggling with: "Am I a healer?"

I am not a "healer." I do my own healing work, and I hold space for others to do their own work. I don't heal people. People heal themselves.

I invest in my own healing and offer support to those who wish to work on their own energy healing. When it comes to working with others, the thing that really connects for me is that the healing isn't mine. I am not doing it nor am I deciding what others should receive. I provide healing support in the same way I coach others. I hold the space, so they can do their own work.

That really speaks to me. Does it speak to you? How does my definition of healing support you? Take a moment now to reflect on what the word "healing" means to you.

Separating from the Whole

You come into the world whole.
Connected to all parts of yourself.
Your mind, heart, body, and spirit inexplicably intertwined.
You cannot tell one part from another part.
At birth, you are one whole person.

Over time, through parenting, education, societal lessons, and a myriad of outside influences, you start to separate. Parts of you become more dominant, and others recede.

I started listening to messages like "be logical" and "don't be so emotional." Gradually, I buried my heart and my spirit in favor of my mind. If it wasn't something I could think through and explain, it wasn't worth pondering. I started explaining my feelings with logic. I started seeing the world and all its humans through judgment. I analyzed everything.

Living with my parts separated, I didn't notice I was disconnected. I'm not sure I would have cared at that time, even if I had known. I forged ahead with a corporate career that rewarded my quick thinking, my analytical mind, and I wasn't asked or expected to bring any other parts of myself. I led from the neck up.

When you think about yourself and your parts, which ones became dominant and which ones receded? Perhaps you can trace the patterns of your own parts through specific events. Or it could be subtler things that took hold over long periods of time.

MY RECEDING HEART

Sometimes the hardest part of healing yourself can be tracing the patterns to those moments when you got hurt. You may not even realize you're carrying those wounds because you tell yourself that everything's fine. You were taught to do this, to just accept that you were born this way, that you can't change, that you don't need healing.

I told myself this story for a long time. I believed that while some children are born athletic, some are not. I believed I was born in that "not" group. Perhaps, also, because my sister was a competitive gymnast and an athlete from birth, I learned to identify as "not an athlete." *Hello, Comparison self.*

I wasn't particularly coordinated. My reflexes were slow, and I was afraid of the ball. These are not exactly ideal characteristics to have when players are being picked for team sports at school. I was always one of the last ones selected. And that hurt, even though I could logically explain why I was chosen last. It made sense to me. But it still hurt.

In grade school, I was tall and lanky. I grew quickly, soon towering over most of the kids in my class. I started puberty early too, growing breasts and getting my period before the other girls. When I was just ten years old, I received an insolent boy's nasty public jeer: "Get a bra!" That stung.

By grade 7, the taunts were meaner and longer lasting. On a few memorable afternoons, a "frenemy" (a friend who was really an enemy), along with her crew of minions, sat on the curb across the street from my house chanting in unison:

"Saggy tits, lots of zits, Heather is a f*cking b*tch."

Those words etched themselves on my heart for a lifetime.

My logical brain could rationalize that this was juvenile behavior, perhaps even a reflection of envy or my frenemy's need to elevate her own status by bringing me down. But my heart ached, and it retreated further into the dark recesses of my core, separating from what was once my whole self. Thus, the warrior self grew stronger and put on heavier armor.

You may remember moments like these in your own life, moments when the foundation cracked, small sharp stabs to the heart that cut away parts of your whole self.

The trouble was, I didn't see it happening because it happened so slowly. I didn't see the breaking up of my whole self. I didn't see me slowly losing my heart. I couldn't see my parts getting split up and shattered. I didn't see the walls I was building to protect those broken parts. I just lifted up my head and kept going.

It's that drive to keep going, keep excelling, keep running on the dreaded treadmill that also keeps you stuck. You need to slow down and stop so you can look around and see what's happening within you.

To start, you can do a quick check-in with your heart. Ask yourself, "What does my heart need in this moment?" If it helps, you can place one hand on your heart when you ask the question. Pay attention to what you hear, and don't judge the answer.

MY RECEDING BODY

Many of my coaching clients share that they struggle with their health. Whether it's their weight, or frequent colds and flus each year, they talk about how their bodies fail them. But are their bodies really failing them? Or are they failing to listen to their bodies?

When your body sends you a message, do you listen?

If you were to rate how connected you are with your own body on a scale of 1 to 10, with 1 being not at all connected and 10 being completely connected, how would you score yourself? If you scored between 7 and 10, you are well connected with your body. If you scored under 7, you may want to tune into your body more.

When I was a decade into my corporate career, I was completely disconnected from my body. If I'd had a scale then, I would have rated myself at -5. I realize now, though, that my body was the last part of me to separate and retreat. I believed that she failed me when I needed her the most.

My belief that I had a weak body started developing in childhood. Not only was I uncoordinated and not athletic, I had countless colds, a long list of allergies, multiple broken bones, and an angry back that flared up at the worst times.

As an adult, my body continued to let me down with continued colds, a C-section that took a longer-than-normal time to heal, sciatica, a torn ACL, a pinched nerve in my shoulder, and most recently, a badly sprained ankle . . . the same one I broke when I was eleven. Each event was proof that my body kept failing me. It never occurred to me that I needed to listen to my body.

While many of these experiences were traumatic, the biggest body challenge I felt I had was with my weight. And I didn't want to talk about it. It was too emotional. The more I thought about it, the more I obsessed over it. The more I obsessed over it, the more I ate crappy food.

How did I get here? At first, I blamed my two pregnancies for the weight. I gained weight because I was pregnant. *Surely that was to be expected. Right?* Except that my comparison self kept comparing me to all the women who didn't end up overweight from pregnancy. I couldn't blame pregnancy.

Next, I blamed my poor eating habits on my busy work schedule, constant travel, and overall exhaustion. I was too tired to make food or go grocery shopping. We ordered in, a lot. Or picked up takeout. I ate Canadian Chinese food (think sweet-and-sour breaded and fried chicken balls with rice) every day for lunch. Every single day!

Then, I started explaining my eating patterns with "I'm an emotional eater." That was true. But somehow when I said it, I was excusing the behavior instead of overcoming it, and my judger self loved it!

It's interesting that only when I look back now do I understand what I couldn't see then. My body never failed me. She was speaking to me. She was crying out and trying to reconnect my broken parts. I just wouldn't listen.

Growing up, I had no one who suggested I pay attention to my body, much less listen to messages she might be sending me. But if you look at it from the whole-self perspective, you can see that my head was explaining what my head thought was happening to my body instead of asking my body what she was trying to say and what she needed.

No matter what you scored on the scale of 1 to 10, I invite you to ask your body what she needs from you in this moment and listen to her answer. Getting into the habit of asking your body what she needs from you is a great way to build a deeper connection with your body—to begin the healing.

Hitting Ground Zero

Sometimes you don't realize you need to work on some self-healing until you hit rock bottom. Other times you pick up on the warning signs before you reach the crisis. It's my hope that you're reading this book before you reach a crisis, but if you're there and starting the journey back from ground zero, know I've got your back, because I've been where you are, and I've learned to love myself. You will too.

I was unhappy for such a long time, and I truly believed unhappiness was normal. I'd accepted that I was destined to be obese and miserable. It was just how being a married, working mom with three young kids was supposed to look. It was the price of focusing on career success.

Did I really believe that, though? I notice how hard it is to ask myself that question and write these words today. I feel the pain in them. My heart hurts for the woman I was then, and I love her so much. Part of healing old wounds is giving them space and grace and accepting that I was doing the best I could. Old me tried so hard to be superwoman. Today, I can love that old version of me, hug her, and set her free. That's part of my healing practice.

I was so disconnected from the parts of myself that knew I was strong and capable.

The "me" at that time was broken.

To the outside world, I had it all: a thriving career at a highly regarded organization and great colleagues I loved working alongside. A happy marriage, three beautiful sons, and a strong extended family network that supported us. Fabulous friends who I adored. Wonderful travel adventures. Weekend skiing throughout the winter.

I checked all the boxes I thought I was supposed to check. So why was I miserable? What was there to be miserable about?

The more miserable I felt, the more weight I gained. The more weight I gained, the more exhausted I felt. The more exhausted I felt, the more disconnected I became. It was a vicious cycle. A roller-coaster ride I couldn't get off.

You know that feeling? Like you're stuck on a roller coaster? Or in a vicious cycle that just keeps spinning? Healing starts with recognizing the current state you're in. Once you can see it, you can start the inner work to heal the parts of yourself that got you here and change or release the stories keeping you stuck.

So, what was my "ground zero" moment when things started to change? It's hard to pinpoint the moment, but I do recall the tough conversation that jolted me awake from my miserable slumber.

I was having lunch with an old colleague and complaining about my weight. She looked at me with love in her eyes and said, "Heather, you can either choose to accept it and stop complaining about it, or you can choose to do something to change it."

Ouch. That really hurt. Sometimes the truth hurts, doesn't it?

She was right, though. I needed to either accept myself as I was or change how I was behaving. It was just the kick in the pants I needed.

Consider a time when you felt like you were spinning or feeling stuck. It could be something alive for you right now, or a time in the past that you remember. Was there a story you were telling yourself that kept you stuck? What's the truth that could create some movement? What do you see now that you didn't see before? What part of you could use some healing?

Hurt

It can often be easier to go through life without stopping to notice there's pain underneath the armor you put on as a warrior. You can charge through life, keeping yourself busy, unaware of the harm it's causing you, or that you're trampling others in your wake.

My warrior energy kept me always in motion. I noticed that I barely journaled at all during the years my warrior self was in full control. Journaling was the one way I could access my heart, and during those warrior years, I didn't want to do that.

But getting to know your warrior helps guide you to the parts of you that could use some attention and possible healing. Exploring where your warrior shows up in your life is a good place to start.

As I did my own inner work, I found it helpful to look back to where my warrior self started taking the lead.

Before my warrior self took over, I had an internal battle going on. When I was a teenager, my inner pain was exposed and raw. I journaled about it daily, but my journaling didn't seem to resolve my pain. It seemed to fuel it. I wore my pain as a badge of honor.

Look how strong I am.
Look how much I can handle.
Look at me.

Reflecting, I can see how trapped my heart was.

I wanted to be loved.
I wanted to be seen.
I wanted attention.

Yet, whenever someone offered love or attention, I fought them with all my might. I pushed people away and rejected any expression of love or care.

I dated a lot in my teens and brought plenty of drama to those relationships. I drew people in, then drove them away to prove I was unlovable. When they left, it was proof I was right. My heart kept searching for love, and my warrior fought to keep me "safe" and alone.

That inner battle occupied me for almost a decade, until finally, the warrior won. She just took over and my heart moved to the basement, hiding in the darkness. By then, I was in my twenties and starting my professional career, so I didn't miss her.

I met my husband, Jason, after the warrior won, and he took on the Herculean effort of loving me, despite all my broken parts. But the hole in my heart prevented me from believing he really loved me. For years, I doubted that his love was real. I couldn't see the hole in my heart, though, because my warrior was fighting and defending my heart at all costs. I believed my doubt was normal, that it was just the way I was, and that he had to work hard to "prove" his love to me. How exhausting!

Once we had children, the hole in my heart only got bigger. I deeply loved my boys, but I constantly doubted they loved me back. It was never enough.

I survived nine years of doubting the love from my sons before I started the journey inward. I survived twelve years of marriage doubting the love of my husband. I survived a lifetime with the hole in my heart before I did the inner work to understand what hurt lay beneath my warrior's protective shield. And what I discovered? It wasn't what I expected.

What might you discover through doing this work? What might be possible? If you're not sure right now, that's okay. Take your time and give yourself space. Connecting with your heart can support you. Be curious and be kind to yourself. You'll find some suggested steps to help you in "Healing as a Practice."

The Healing Begins

Sometimes healing starts without you noticing it. You can be guided by your heart, by another kind soul, or by the universe, but it's only when things start to change that you realize healing is happening. In other instances, you make the conscious choice to start your own healing process.

Today, in reflection, I can see the moment my healing began. Even though I wasn't looking for it or consciously choosing it, my heart and the universe had other plans. It was 2012 and I thought I'd ticked all the boxes based on my definition of "success." We had it all. Yet, I wasn't happy. I was miserable.

I was overweight and exhausted all the time, *and* I was short-tempered and impatient with everyone. I was striving for "more," but I didn't know what more was, and I kept looking outward to find it.

I blamed my weight.
I blamed my kids.
I blamed my husband.
I blamed my job.
I blamed a variety of external reasons for my unhappiness.
I never once thought of looking inward.

After the uncomfortable but necessary comment from my colleague, I decided to take a week off to be by myself. It was April, and I had the freedom of feeling no guilt for missing work, as I had an extra week of vacation time banked. So, I planned a "staycation" where the kids went to school, my husband went to work, and I had the days entirely to myself.

On the first day, I dropped the kids off at school and felt immense delight wash over me.

What am I going to do today? I decided to go to my favorite bookstore first. I planned to explore the shelves, pick out a few books, buy myself a latte, and read without distraction for a couple hours.

As I drove to the bookstore in the sunshine, I felt as if it were shining just for me. Then, the perfect spot sat open in the parking lot as if it had been waiting for my use. (Usually, the lot was packed, and I'd spend ages looking to park.) *Amazing.*

I walked into the bookstore with a lightness in my step. The joy from having a day of freedom intensified. As I rode the escalator to the second floor, I eyed the sections of books around the room. My eyes caught the Self-Help section. I sighed. *More shelf-help,* I thought. *Just what I need.*

Without the usual rush to pick up a specific title or being pulled by small hands to the kids' section, I let my eyes lead me to the shelves of self-help books. There, one suddenly caught my attention. I heard a small *yes* that seemed to come from somewhere deep within me.

"Pardon?" I looked around.

Yes, the voice whispered again.

I picked up the book and felt what I can only describe as an electrical current surging from my fingertips through my body to my toes.

Yes.

This book focused on the relationship between hormones and diet. I was curious about the book, about why this and why now.

I had never liked the word "diet," yet I knew I needed to do something about my health and, specifically, my weight. I felt extremely resistant toward the idea of denying myself anything. Yet, I held this "diet" book in my hands and felt compelled to read it. *How curious!*

Listening to the quiet voice inside me, I purchased the book, then headed to the coffee shop in the bookstore to buy my favorite indulgence: a grande vanilla latte. With drink in hand, I found a little nook and opened the book to a random page that contained a list of symptoms. As I read the list, I noted that I had every single one of them. For the first time in a long time, I felt a glimmer of hope.

After years of tests and visits to doctors to try and find out why I was always so tired, why I was often in pain, why my hair was falling out, and why I often felt sick after eating, might this book finally have the answers I had been seeking? I couldn't read it quickly enough.

The book was more about balancing my hormones than it was about being on a diet. Just balancing my hormones could bring me relief from the health issues I'd struggled with since I was a teenager, and I didn't need to take medication to do it. *Amazing.*

My heart danced with joy as I embraced the possibility of a different way to feel, a different way to live. I thanked the universe for the message and the gift. I could feel my heart smiling along with my mouth as I settled in to absorb all the wisdom I could from this book in my hands.

I didn't know it yet, but that was the moment I started living by heart.

Could this moment—right now—be the moment you start your own journey to healing, to living by heart? Where would you want to start? Take a moment to check in with your heart. Ask: "What part of me could use some healing?"

Note: You need to be kind to yourself and patient. It took years to break down your various parts and hide them away. Doing the healing work on yourself isn't something you do just once. It takes patience and daily practice. (In "Healing as a Practice," I'll share tips for building your own daily healing practice.)

Space to Heal

At this point you may be thinking, *I didn't know this was going to be a book on improving eating habits.*

Don't worry—it isn't.

Living by HEART is about how healing one part of yourself can start a chain reaction of healing within you. For me, what began as a journey to balance my hormones started a chain reaction through my whole being. It was my body that needed healing first, and by healing my body, I got inspired to keep working on healing the rest of myself. It's important for you to check in with yourself to identify which part of you is the best place to begin.

When I started, I asked questions to see which part of myself would answer:

What does my body need right now?
What does my heart need right now?
What does my spirit need right now?

Ask yourself these questions, and if you hear your mind answer, thank her and ask that she step aside so you can listen to and hear from the other parts of yourself.

As I've shared, I heard my body answer first. She told me she needed me to pay close attention to her. So, I did.

After completing a two-week detox, I noticed how different I felt. I had more energy. The brain fog disappeared. I felt more emotionally balanced.

And healing my body by nourishing it with good food was just the beginning. The better my body and my mind felt, the more curious I became. Seeing improvements in how I felt in my body made me want to see results everywhere right away. I wanted more, *now*. And I had the energy to do the work! *What else can I work on?*

How about some physical exercise? my body suggested.

Oh, I don't think so, my judger self replied.

Why not? It will feel good, my body urged.

I don't do exercise! My judger self was firm!

True. You don't do it today but could you? my body asked with playful curiosity as she stretched her limbs.

Humph, huffed my judger self.

Could it be possible? I felt strong resistance to the idea. But it kept percolating.

In June 2012, Jason and our oldest son decided to run in the Toronto 5 km race. It was our son's first time running in an organized street race outside of school events. He was excited. Jason was excited too, and I was excited for them.

On race day, I stood on the sidelines and cheered as they ran past me. Then I hustled to the finish line so I could be there to greet them when they completed their first race together.

As I watched for them to turn the corner and head down the final stretch of road, I heard a little voice inside me whisper *yes.*

Yes what?
Yes, you can run with them.
What?! That's crazy. I can't run.
What if you can?

I shook my head. But I couldn't deny that in my heart I wanted to be running with them.

I want to run.

Unraveling the First Story

In the Introduction, I discussed how inner work is about unraveling. It's about uncovering the stories that are keeping you stuck, exploring them, healing the hurt underneath them, and writing new stories.

If you have started this work already, and you know you have a story that's keeping you stuck, feel free to follow along by unraveling your story as I share the first big story that I unraveled: "I Can't Run."

First, let's look at the root of where the story began. My "I Can't Run" story started when I was eight years old.

My sister and I begged our parents to bring home a kitten from a farm we were visiting. They said yes, and shortly after we brought Fluffy home, we discovered that I was allergic to cats. My doctor wanted to see what else I might be allergic to, so she recommended I get an allergy test. I didn't know anything about how doctors test someone for allergies, so it sounded like a great idea.

I vividly remember the day I got tested. The allergist had racks of vials set up on the counter beside the medical table. After I changed into a hospital gown, she instructed me to lie down on my stomach on the table and to stay still. I remember wondering how they were going to test for so many different allergens. I also remember wondering just how many things a person could be allergic to.

The allergist placed a drop of liquid from each vial on my back, fifty in total, then proceeded to prick one at a time. "If you're allergic to something, the spot on your skin will react. You might feel a little bit itchy."

Almost immediately, my back was itchy everywhere. It was impossible to stay still, but I did my best while the allergist noted which drops I'd reacted to. The test confirmed I was allergic to cats. It also confirmed that I was allergic to all animals with fur or feathers, all grasses, plus trees, weeds, hay, dust, pollen, and mold. It felt like I was allergic to the world.

On my next visit to my family doctor, I was prescribed a daily antihistamine pill, a monthly allergy shot, and a Ventolin inhaler because I had allergic asthma. And with that Ventolin inhaler, my story began: "I can't run."

And here's how my story grew into a "truth."

At school, we were training for the upcoming cross-country meet. During every gym class, we would exit the school and use the neighborhood streets to train for the 2 km race.

I'd always felt a tightness in my chest when I tried to run long distances. Now, with asthma, my mind got the better of me. Whenever I'd start to run, I felt panic set in. I couldn't breathe. I had asthma. My Ventolin inhaler became a badge of honor. Each time we left the school grounds to run, I would panic, then use my inhaler and start walking. After a few gym classes, panic, and tears, my gym teacher exempted me from running. After that, every year in September, I informed the new gym teacher that I had asthma and couldn't run. So began my life on the bench.

Think about one of your stories. If you're feeling a little uncomfortable at this point, that's normal. Unraveling a story you've been carrying, especially for years, *can* be uncomfortable. When you break down the pieces of the story and explore the moment the story was created, you might discover the story isn't true or that it no longer applies. Unraveling stories brings judgment. Your inner critic loves when you doubt yourself and unraveling can create doubt. If this story you've been carrying isn't true, what does that say about you? That's your inner critic talking. Notice her. Remember that you're unraveling a story, so be kind to yourself. Try to focus on the facts and feelings and not judge yourself along the way.

You may also experience some fear at this point too. I felt fear when I realized my "I Can't Run" story wasn't based on evidence. Instead, it was based on an assumption I'd made that when my chest tightened up as a kid from running, it was the same as the asthma I experienced when I was having an allergic reaction. A natural assumption for a child to make. So, how could I overcome that fear to test whether the theory was true?

TESTING THE STORY

After seeing the joy on Jason's and our son's face when they finished their race, I wanted to run. But how could I? The story "I Can't Run" was deeply embedded in my mind and I had proof. I'd tried to run years earlier and failed. I had asthma.

That was my story, but now that I was nourishing my body, many other old stories I'd believed to be true had been proven wrong. So much had changed just from doing one thing differently. I wondered what else might be possible.

To challenge my "I Can't Run" story, I signed up for a women's run/walk program. The first day was on a cool September Sunday morning. I could see my breath when I stepped out of my car and walked toward the group of women stretching and laughing together. I was terrified. I wanted to hop back in my car and drive home before the class even began.

The instructor smiled as I approached, her warmth inviting me to join the group of strangers. She asked what our levels of running experience were, and I was the only beginner. The instructor then asked us to state our goals, and at the time, my only goal was to not die running on the first day.

We started with an "easy" run called One and Fours: one minute running followed by four minutes walking for a total of twenty minutes of exercise. It seemed to me that the other women in the group started without any difficulty.

Running for one minute straight was a big challenge for me. After about fifteen seconds, I started to panic, and I felt my chest constricting. *How could I possibly complete a whole minute?!* The instructor suddenly appeared beside me.

"You've got this," she said and smiled.

I shook my head, not wanting to waste any air trying to talk.

"You're holding your breath," she said. "Remember to breathe." I didn't know I wasn't breathing. I tried to take a breath. It felt more like a gasp.

"That's it. Ten seconds left. Eight, seven, six . . . one more breath . . . three, two, one. Now, walk for four minutes. You did it!"

I did it! I had run for one solid minute. It was hard, but I did it.

Four minutes later, it was time to run again for one minute.

I was scared, but I was a little less scared than I had been the first minute. I paid attention to my breathing, and while it was difficult, I gasped less.

At the end of the first twenty-minute exercise, I celebrated running for four whole minutes—something I never thought I could do. The women cheered and celebrated with me. Maybe "I Can't Run" wasn't true at all.

I continued with the run/walk program through the fall of that year, and in late November, I ran my first 5 km race, "The Santa Shuffle." Instead of standing on the sidelines and cheering for my family, it was me running across the finish line while cheering for myself!

Find a way to test your story. Whether it's a class, a conversation, or another kind of challenge. Identify one small way to test whatever the story is that's holding you so tightly.

If I could run for one minute, I could run. I didn't have to prove I could run by running a 5 km race on the first day. All I had to do was test the story. Choose one way you want to test your own story, to see where it might lead you.

Hole in My Heart

Nourishing my body with food and learning to run busted some long-standing beliefs I had about myself. I had created space for healing. What else did I want to work on?

Journaling can be a useful tool for identifying and unraveling your stories. When I started living by heart, I found myself journaling daily again. If you've never journaled, I encourage you to give it a try. You can ask yourself a single question like "What's a story I'm holding on to?" to figure out what you want to unravel next and see what shows up.

For example, here's an excerpt from a journal entry that started unraveling the hole in my heart. I asked myself one question: "What do I want?"

I want to feel loved.
I want to feel cherished, adored, even worshipped.
I want to feel worthy.
I want to feel needed.
I want to feel valued and appreciated.
I want to feel respected.

These felt like things I had wanted my whole life, going as far back as I could remember. At least, that was the story I told myself—that I was "always wanting." The truth is, most of my childhood memories are filled with love, happiness, and laughter. So, how did that story of "wanting" start?

SEARCHING FOR THE ROOT OF THE STORY

When you discover new insights that seem to have an "always" or "never" attached to them, it's a good indication that there's a story to unravel. You may not need to go back into childhood memories; it all depends on when the story started. Some stories are built in adulthood and don't require searching in the memory banks for moments in your childhood.

In this case, the story of "always wanting" compelled me to look for the root of the story in some of my earliest memories. Why did I think I was "always wanting"?

Reflecting on my childhood memories, I discovered that "wanting" wasn't part of them. Instead, I found memories of warm summers spent in Maine at the ocean with my family and friends. Memories of long car rides while playing games together like "I Spy with My Little Eye," picnics at the beach, and eating breakfast out of small cereal boxes cut open and filled with milk, right there in the box.

I found memories of winter vacations spent skiing with my parents, sister, and cousins, of sleigh rides, skating on the lake, and giggling together at the dinner table.

While I searched for the root of my story that I was "always wanting," I didn't find any evidence in my childhood memories. I had to admit that the first assumption that had created this story was inaccurate. I wasn't "always wanting."

If you have a story that includes an "always" or "never" in it, take the time to explore whether that absolute is valid.

FINDING THE ROOT

Once the absolute of "always" was removed from my story of wanting, I was curious to find the root of the story. I knew it wasn't in any of my childhood memories from birth to ten years old. I do know that when my parents separated just before my tenth birthday, however, something in me changed. I lost my certainty that love was forever. I lost my belief that I knew what love looked like.

The evening my parents told my sister and me they were separating is etched in my memory.

Mom and Dad sat us down. They both looked upset and uncomfortable, but they tried to maintain their composure. I could feel the sadness emanating from my mother. I felt fear, and a lump formed in my throat. My dad started talking first.

"Mom and I have something to tell you—"

"And we want you to know how much we love you," Mom said, jumping in.

"Your mother and I have decided to separate," Dad said plainly.

My mom winced. I wanted to jump off the couch and hug her, but my fear kept me frozen in my seat.

"Why?" I asked.

"While we both love you, we no longer love each other."

I don't remember who said this last part, but the words stung and echoed in my ears years after they were uttered. I still hear them.

I have no memories of what happened that day after those words were said. I am sure I cried. I am sure I tried to argue, debate, convince them they were wrong. But I wasn't present in my body after I heard the words "we no longer love each other." How could love be so fickle? How could it just disappear one day without any advance notice?

Years later I'd learn that it didn't end in a moment. It had been slowly dying over the years, but I didn't know that or see it.

I don't know if I loved myself before that day. I do know that I doubted receiving love from anyone else after that day. I know that I didn't feel loved after that day, despite deeply wanting to feel loved. So, I started looking for love.

This is also the moment my warrior self first stood up and took charge. I was the warrior for myself. I was the warrior for my mom. I started feeding the warrior, and my big heart stood back to let her take the lead.

Just six months after they separated, my parents reconciled. I don't know whether they did it for us, for themselves, or both. I do know that things seemed better. Vacations, holidays, and all the things I worried about losing when they split up were back to normal. But while it was better for me, it wasn't better for them. Ten years later, they divorced.

Let me tell you, I've really struggled with the notion that my parents' separation broke something in me. I've resisted it. I didn't want to blame an external event for anything that happened to me. I wasn't a victim. My warrior self could never accept that I could be a victim, under any circumstances. I told myself the hole in my heart wasn't caused by that moment. I was certain of it.

Now, I'm not so sure. It's possible that the event did create a break within me. That can be true, and it doesn't make me a victim. Unless I let it.

Being a victim, or seeing myself as a victim, is a choice. The event occurred and it was outside of my control. In fact, a lot of experiences happened in the six months after my parents separated that changed me. It took me a long time to accept that this event could be the moment that broke my heart, and it was then that I started feeling unloved and unworthy.

As you explore the root of your story, you may struggle with what you uncover. Know you always have a choice. Be curious, be kind, and be patient with yourself. Pause and give yourself space.

Note: If at any time it feels too heavy or too hard to work through this type of testing on your own, ask for help. The inner work of healing can bring up emotions, judgment, and parts of yourself that could use more support than your own healing practice.

REALIZING THE ROOT OF THE STORY

You may find as you work on unraveling your stories and healing that your understanding of yourself changes along the way. Each time you unravel a story and heal from long-held beliefs, you change.

In the early years of my living by heart journey, I believed I had a hole in my heart that needed to be filled. I've since learned that my heart has always been whole, she was just buried deep and protected by my warrior self.

In 2014 I wrote a speech for a Toastmasters contest entitled "(W)Hole in My Heart." I liked the play on words—that I initially had a hole in my heart, and through this journey I had reached a point of feeling whole in my heart.

It was a speech about my not feeling loved and not being enough, then the realization that the only way I could receive love from others was if I first learned to love myself. When I wrote it, I was really focused on my healing journey and repairing the hole in my heart. I wasn't interested in or even curious about how the hole got there.

I spoke about being born with a hole in my heart. Here was the long-held belief that I was born wanting, even without any evidence.

The story I'd been carrying for years was:
I craved love from the womb.
I don't remember ever feeling loved enough.
I don't remember ever feeling liked enough.
I don't remember ever feeling that I was enough.

When I delivered my speech, though, other people heard in it that the hole formed when my parents separated. I'd never thought about it that way. It had never felt like there was an event that had created the hole in my heart. I just assumed it had always been there. I don't hold any hurt or blame toward my parents at all. What other people were seeing as an obvious connection, I just didn't.

That said, these insights led me to reflect on the day my parents told me they were separating. I had to admit it was significant. As I shared, it's the moment I started questioning what love looked like. It's the moment I asked myself questions like:

How will I know love is real if it can suddenly disappear just like that? Can someone love me and then suddenly leave me?

When I first wrote down my feelings and those questions on paper, I could see what other people had been talking about. While I couldn't admit my parents' separation may have caused the hole in my heart, I could see how it impacted my trust in love.

As you read the unraveling of my story, how does it impact you and the story you're currently unraveling? You may want to give yourself time to write down the reflections for your own story and explore the root of it. See if writing it down brings new insights for you.

EXPLORING THE STORY

You may sometimes start working on healing a part of yourself before you know the root of the story. You don't have to start at the root, especially if searching for it is frustrating or you feel strong resistance to it. You can start anywhere. If you know there's a story currently getting in your way, you may choose to work from this point forward instead of searching for the root.

As a coach, I work with clients on their current state, then moving toward their desired future state. We seldom go back to the root of the story in our work together; the client may choose to do that work on their own or with a trained professional. What we work on together is the gap between where they are now and where they want to be.

In 2012, two years before the speech and the insights that occurred as a result, I started working inward. I desperately wanted to feel the love I knew Jason and the boys had for me. I desperately wanted to know love in my heart. I desperately wanted to feel like I was enough.

I didn't know how to make that happen.

At first, I thought I needed to know what caused me to feel that way. I asked myself a lot of questions, exploring my childhood and teenage years, seeking to understand the source of my "wanting."

The more questions I asked myself, the more questions I had. It was frustrating and felt futile. Then, I discovered some better questions to ask:

What was missing that I needed to feel loved?
What did it mean to feel like enough?
Why wasn't my love for myself enough?

That last question really struck a nerve.

An inner dialogue started:

What do you mean, love for me?
Well, what if the love you have for yourself was enough to sustain you?
What if I don't have any love for myself?
Ah, my love. This is where you need to start.

By focusing on the current state and what I wanted, I discovered what I needed to heal and what I needed to work on. I needed to build love for myself. The hole in my heart couldn't be filled by

Jason's deep love for me. It couldn't be filled by the hugs, kisses, and cuddles from my three affectionate sons. It couldn't be filled by friends or family, by colleagues or clients. The only one who could fill the hole in my heart was me.

Ouch.

Earlier in the Introduction, I talked about the surface work and the deeper inner work. The surface work is where you begin. It is understanding what your feelings are, whether you feel unworthy, or unloved, or not loved enough, or something else entirely. The deeper work is looking at what's really going on now, determining where you want to be or how you want to feel, and choosing what you'll work on to get there.

The healing work begins with unraveling the stories keeping you stuck. When you can get to the root of the story, explore what's true and what you can let go of, then start creating a new story.

Whole in My Heart

When you've unraveled your story and know what you want to work on, you can start the work toward your desired future state.

Once I recognized I was the only one who could fill the hole in my heart, I focused on ways to build my love for myself. It wasn't easy. As I share some of the work I did to build love for myself, I invite you to consider which activities might work best to support you.

For today, I love myself.

Some people collect cars. Some people collect shoes, or stamps, or art. I love collecting two things: books and decks of oracle cards. I collect books because I love to learn, and every time I attend a conference, webinar, or workshop, I add the recommended books to my wish list. Jason says I'm a book hoarder. He's not entirely wrong.

I love using oracle cards to ground my energy, guide my actions, and most importantly, set my intentions for the day. One of my favorite decks is *Seeds of Intention: Daily Intentions for Living on Purpose* by Adrienne Enns. Each card begins with the words "For today . . ."

I love this language. Setting an intention for one day allows me to be present in the moment and removes any pressure that I must do something every day or forever. Instead, I can delight in doing something just for today.

In the beginning, the idea of loving myself was extremely uncomfortable. I felt like a fraud. I felt guilty. Who am I to be deserving of love?

Who are you not to be? my heart answered.

Loving myself felt like bragging or conceit. I worried I'd become full of myself. Arrogant even.

Love, you can love yourself and love others.
I can?
Yes, love.
Okay. Maybe just for today, I can love myself.
That's a great place to start.

My heart didn't heal overnight. Yours won't either. It takes patience, commitment, and kindness for yourself.

The commitment to love myself just for today was only part of the inner work. I also started a daily journaling practice that included morning and evening reflections.

Each morning, I asked, "How will I love myself today?"

This helped me set some intentions for ways I could show myself love throughout the day. I already had some loving practices in place, such as loving myself by eating nourishing food and running or going to a yoga class. I discovered that reading a book or watching a favorite TV show uninterrupted were ways I could show myself love too. Listening to music, getting together with friends, and singing every day were ways I could honor and love myself as well.

There were certainly times when I felt guilty doing some of these activities, but now I had tools to remind me that I could love myself *and* love others. I didn't have to choose one over the other. I could make time for both.

Each evening, I asked, "How did I love myself today?"

On some days I noted several things I'd purposely done to love myself. On other days I noticed I hadn't done anything to love myself. I looked for patterns I could reinforce and patterns I could break to love myself more each day. And the more work I did on myself, the more I seemed to attract other people who were doing their own inner work.

During my inner work, I came across an activity called "Mirror Work" that made me feel really uncomfortable. I didn't want to do it, but now that I was paying attention to my feelings, I realized my discomfort must be a sign that I needed to do it.

Just the word "mirror" made me uncomfortable. I didn't like looking at myself in the mirror. Whenever I looked, a flurry of self-criticisms flooded my thoughts. How could I sit and just look at myself?

This assignment required me to look at myself in the mirror and *only* see the good.
How? It's not possible.
My heart replied with curiosity. *What if it's great?*
What if it hurts?
What if it helps?
What if I cry?
What if you do?

I took a deep breath, closed the door for some privacy, and sat down in front of the full-length mirror in my bedroom. "Just for today, I will look at myself with love."

At first, all I saw were the things I wanted to change about myself. I took another deep breath.

"I love you," I said to the face looking back at me. She winced.
"I love you," I repeated. This time her eyes welled up with tears.
"I love you," I choked out a third time. Now the tears flowed steadily.

I watched the woman before me release her emotions freely. How beautiful.

I observed the rosy glow in her cheeks.
I observed the gentle, encouraging smile flit across her lips.
I observed her loving, caring eyes looking back at me.
I felt her love.
An exchange between my reflection and me.
An energy surging with compassion, kindness, and a strength I'd never felt before.

This feeling of strength was so very different from the warrior energy I'd gotten used to carrying. This strength came from deep in my soul and, at the same time, I felt connected with the whole universe. It was a feeling of oneness, a feeling of wholeness.

Whole in my heart, where there once had been a hole in my heart. This is where self-love lives.

What stands out to you in this story? How could using intention cards, journaling, or mirror work help you connect with your heart and build your self-love? Take some time now to reflect on what might work best for you and if you want, write down your thoughts.

Whole Healing

What happens when you learn to love yourself? The short answer is, everything changes. When you learn to love yourself, you see the world differently. You experience love from others differently. You give love and receive love differently. Loving yourself is the foundation of all transformation. When you love yourself, you can start working on other limiting beliefs like feeling unworthy or feeling like you're not enough.

As I learned to love myself and fill the hole in my heart, I was able to give and receive love more freely. Loving myself and pouring into my own "love cup" filled the void I'd been seeking to fill externally for years. It took the pressure off my husband and my kids to "make me feel loved."

It hurts me to look back on the years I sought love externally. I see the impact I had on my marriage and the pressure I placed on Jason to fill my love cup. When he failed to love me enough, I blamed him and expected him to change.

In filling my own love cup, I receive his love without doubt or judgment. He doesn't have to change a thing. His love is more than enough. He is more than enough.

I see the impact I had on my relationship with my sons. I used to constantly hug them, kiss them, and tell them I loved them—with the expectation that they hugged and kissed me and said I love you back. I smothered them, trying to feel love back from them.

In filling my own love cup, I no longer expect hugs, kisses, and love from my boys. I give to them generously from my love cup, which is overflowing. I'm not attached to or expecting any reciprocity. My actions are to make sure they feel loved by me. Now that they are young men, instead of my three small boys, I appreciate and openly receive any form of love they choose to show, when they show it.

Having filled my own "love cup," having become whole in my heart, I see the world completely differently. My heart was right: I can love myself and love others too.

So can you.

I Am Worthy

What does it mean to feel worthy? What does it mean to feel like you're enough?

When I start working with a new client, often one of the first things they mention is a feeling of "not enough." It's so common that I started assuming everyone suffers from a feeling of unworthiness. That's not true, though. It can be dangerous to think in absolutes and assume that "everyone" experiences anything universally.

Understanding your own sense of worthiness requires curiosity. If you're confident, people may assume you don't doubt yourself. If you're shy or timid, people may assume you lack self-confidence and have a high level of self-doubt. But we can't tell whether someone else feels worthy without asking them.

You can't fully assess your own sense of worthiness without asking all parts of yourself. I made the mistake early on of only asking my warrior self, and I'm sure you can imagine her answer.

My warrior self likes to protect me from showing any signs of what she perceives as weakness. I've had to do a lot of work to tame her and get her to relax out there on the swings for a while when I'm working on my worthiness.

Over the years, I've done a lot of work on feeling worthy. I've worked on my own through journaling, meditation, and mirror work. I've also engaged other practitioners to support me. Whether through Reiki, Tao Hands, EFT (Emotional Freedom Technique) tapping, or breathwork, each modality has helped me access deeper parts of my self-doubt and feelings of unworthiness.

I'm always amazed there's still more work to do and that new emotions surface each time I focus on my own self-worth. The journey never ends.

For example, one EFT session stands out in my memory. I'd just started working with a new EFT practitioner, Arielle. I felt excited and skeptical at the same time, as often happens when I work with someone new.

I came to the EFT session with two clear topics I wanted to focus on: First, I wanted more energy to get through all that I had on my plate, and second, I wanted to work on my relationship with money.

After a bit of discussion, we decided to work on my relationship with money. Arielle invited me to talk about my relationship with money and where I felt I needed to do some work. What was the barrier or challenge I was facing? How did I want to feel in my relationship with money?

As we explored what I wanted, the connection to my worthiness in the world showed up (again), and that was where the real inner work began.

I've participated in EFT sessions in the past. Many, in fact. I know that when you are tapping into something within you that can use some healing, emotions can easily surface. I often cry during EFT sessions, so I was ready for that.

I wasn't ready for the response I had when Arielle guided me.

She started with me tapping on my hand. "Repeat after me," she said. And with the very first sentence out of her mouth, I started to laugh. Each new sentence she invited me to say, I giggled harder. By the time we were really into the first round of tapping, I was laughing uncontrollably. I couldn't stop. I could barely breathe. The words came out in gasps for air. I was laughing so hard that tears were streaming out of my eyes. *Well, here are the tears I was expecting.*

I really couldn't stop laughing. My body didn't feel like my own. The laughter just kept coming and it was such a powerful release of energy. I was shocked. I had never had that kind of response before. I felt my inner critic judging me. *What the hell is wrong with you?! Stop laughing.*

After round one of the tapping was done, I tried to settle down, but each time I thought I was getting calm, laughs would escape from me again.

I apologized to Arielle. "I'm so sorry. I don't know why I'm laughing so much. I can't seem to stop it."

Arielle invited me to accept whatever emotions or physical reactions were showing up.

There's still more, I heard my heart say. *Just let it go.*

Arielle asked me to rate my sense of unworthiness, and I was at an 8 as I had been when we'd begun. I wished I could tell her it had improved. I wanted to say the tapping was helping, but my heart knew that I was still feeling unworthy and that more work was needed.

We started round two of the tapping. I started laughing again. It was less maniacal this time, but still strong. I could feel the releasing of energy I had been holding on to so tightly. I felt the story begin to unravel. I could feel my curiosity engage and a desire to start doing the deeper healing work laid open before me. The laughing slowly tapered off as we proceeded through the tapping exercise.

Then she said the words that triggered the floodgate of emotions:

"I am worthy."

My whole body tightened with resistance, my voice suddenly small and scared.

"I am worthy," I croaked out.

"I am worthy," she said again, powerful and with confidence.

"I am worthy." My inner critic cringed as I repeated the words. I felt like I wanted to curl up in a ball and hide.

"I am worthy," Arielle said.

Oh god, why is this so difficult for me?

"I am worthy," I repeated, still timid but less cringy. The tightness in my body had relaxed just a little.

"I am worthy."

"I am worthy." I felt my back straighten as I said it that time. The first tears crested the edge of both eyes.

"I am worthy." Man, she knew she'd hit a nerve as this exercise continued.

"I am worthy," I said, sobbing now. The floodgates had fully opened as I knew they would.

"I am worthy."

"I am worthy," I said as my judger self, trying to control the narrative, cried out: *No, you're not!*

"I am worthy."

Wow! There is so much here that I need to unpack.

"I am worthy." More tears.

"I am worthy."

"I am worthy." My heart shifted a bit, and I felt the sun streaming in through my window onto my tear-stained face as if to say, *You are loved.*

We came out of the tapping and took a few deep breaths.

I felt different. I felt lighter. *Impossible!* claimed my judger self.

You are worthy, my love. You have always been worthy, claimed my heart.

I could feel a broad smile creep across my face. I have always been worthy. Yes, there was a powerful knowing that it was true within me. A sense of calm washed over me like a warm, cozy blanket you never want to climb out from under. I felt peace.

There is so much work to do on my own sense of worthiness, even though I feel like I have already done so much. It is a nev-er-ending practice to love, nurture, and care for my own heart.

Note: If you're curious about EFT tapping, you may want to book a session to explore your own worthiness or sense of self-love. If you do, I encourage you to seek a certified EFT practitioner.

For now, I ask that you do a quick activity to build your own worthiness:

Put one hand on your heart and the other hand on your gut, just below your belly button. You can close your eyes or keep them open—whatever feels most comfortable. When you feel ready, say "I am worthy" out loud. Notice if you feel any resistance or judgment. You can shake it off by shaking out your hands and then returning them to your heart and your gut.

Say it out loud again, slowly this time. "I am worthy."

Sit up tall with your back straight and shoulders back. Take a deep cleansing breath if you want to. Then say it one more time. "I am worthy."

When you finish, take a moment to reflect. How did it feel? What did you notice? How do you feel about your own worthi-ness? Notice if the exercise was easy or felt difficult. A simple practice like this one can help guide you to the work you may want to do on your own feelings of worthiness.

Healing as a Practice

A quick reminder that self-healing may stir up emotions. Check in with yourself to make sure you feel safe, that you feel supported, and that you feel ready to go deeper into your own inner work. If you don't, take a pause and be sure to get professional support if you need it.

Once you've checked in with yourself and feel ready to do some inner work, here are a few practices I recommend:

SELF-REFLECTION:

To uncover where you may have opportunities for self-healing, the work begins with self-reflection. Think of it like holding up a mirror so you can see yourself as you really are. Some curious questions to ask:

What areas of my life could use some healing?

How connected am I to my heart right now?

How do I listen to my heart?

There are many forms of self-reflection available to you. If you already have a self-reflection practice in place that works well, continue using it. If you don't, test out the various options and find the one that works best for you.

Journaling – This is my favorite form of self-reflection, not only because I love to write but also because journaling provides me with an easy way to spot patterns of thinking or feeling and then work through them. Choose a time in the day that works best for you and try to journal regularly. This isn't about perfection. You don't need to journal every day or feel bad if you miss one. Journaling regularly helps build a habit. You will gain more insight from consistently journaling than if you do it sparingly.

Meditating – This form of self-reflection can be helpful to calm the mind, align the body, and check in with your heart. There are numerous resources to help you build a meditation practice, so find a resource to support you if you're new to meditation. And don't worry if you struggle to "clear your mind." Everyone does when they first get started.

Walking – This form of self-reflection is particularly helpful for people who think best when they're moving. You want to be sure that you are connecting with your heart and your body before you begin your walk. Taking a few deep breaths and stretching before you begin can be helpful. If you want to capture your thoughts while you're walking, try using the voice memo feature on your phone and talk while you walk.

DAILY SELF-REFLECTION:

Once you've uncovered the area(s) you want to work on, use the self-reflection practice daily with questions like:

Morning:
How will I show myself love today?
What do I need to support my heart today?

Evening:
How did I show myself love today?
What intentions do I want to set for loving myself tomorrow?

Take a moment to jot down some daily questions that would be most helpful for you to ask yourself.

MIRROR WORK:

This activity sounds simple, yet it isn't easy. The more times you do mirror work, the easier it gets and the faster you connect with your own self-love energy.

Ensure that you have a space where you can have some privacy and a mirror that is mounted or standing on something so you don't need to hold it up. I don't recommend using your phone's camera for this exercise. You want to turn off all technology and be present with only your own reflection in the mirror.

You'll also want to give yourself some time for this exercise. I recommend twenty to thirty minutes, but if you're uncomfortable, start with five minutes and work your way up to twenty.

Take time to just look at yourself. Don't say anything. Look at yourself with love. If it helps, put one hand on your heart so you can connect with it for this exercise. Notice if you want to look away. Bring your eyes back to your reflection and breathe.

Imagine you're breathing out judgment and breathing in love. You can silently connect with your heart by using a mantra like "Look with love. Look with love." Or you may wish to silently ask yourself, "What does my heart see?"

As you look at yourself, notice if you're criticizing your flaws or appreciating your features. If it feels appropriate, use loving language to speak out loud to yourself. You could say, "I love you" if that feels useful. You could also look at specific features and say, "I love my [note a feature] because [say what you love about it]."

You can also use the mirror for the "I Am Worthy" activity you did earlier. Instead of closing your eyes, look at yourself in the mirror and repeat "I am worthy" five to six times slowly. Be sure to take at least one complete breath between each statement. Notice how your reflection responds when you say it.

EMPATHY

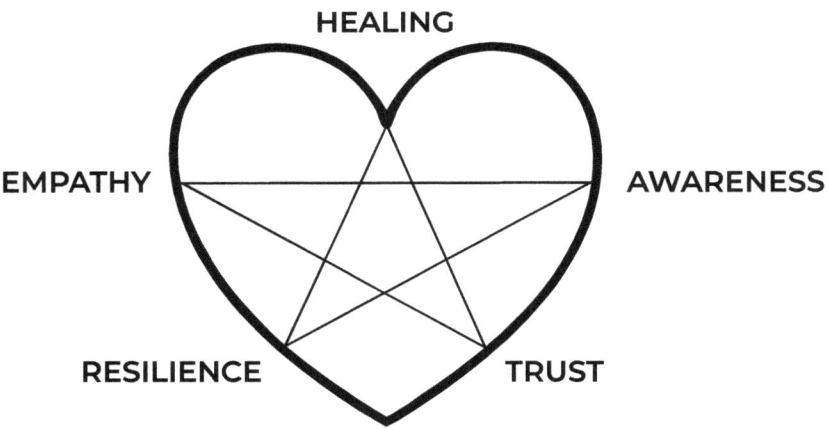

What Is Empathy?

Empathy is holding space for others, accepting them as they are, and sitting with them quietly without judgment. It's an important skill, both in work and in life.

Empathy was once seen as a "soft skill" in the workplace, but the COVID crisis helped organizations recognize just how important empathy was to employee engagement and well-being. Today, empathy is no longer seen as a "nice to have" soft skill; instead, it is a vital "must-have" skill.

When I started delivering training on empathy, I was struck by how easy it was to talk about empathy and how hard it was to model what empathy looked like in action. I also discovered that many people confuse empathy with sympathy.

Researcher and author Brené Brown has an excellent YouTube video in which she talks about empathy versus sympathy. (See Resources section at back of book for a link to the video.) It really helped me distinguish between what empathy and sympathy look like in action.

Many people know what empathy is and think knowing what it is and being empathetic are the same thing. They understand empathy in theory, they may even know some empathetic language, but most people aren't very good at it. That's because empathy takes practice.

You can tell people that you care about them and their situation and do your best to actively listen when they speak, but embodying empathy requires you to really *be* with someone. It requires you to hold space for them, and sit with them, often silently, without judgment. And that can be uncomfortable.

So, when it comes to living by heart, you need to embody empathy.

Discovering the importance of empathy in living by heart came as a surprise to me. When I started doing inner work in 2012, I never imagined it would lead me into working on my empathy. It seemed counterintuitive. Why would doing work on myself and the pain I was carrying require me to develop empathy for others?

I wasn't trying to be "more" for people. I already felt over-whelmed and tended to overextend myself to others, often at my own expense. Why would I want to focus on other people more?

I focused on the "inside job" to make myself feel healthier, happier, and in greater harmony in my own work and life. But the parts of me that kept surfacing, my judger self and warrior self, needed empathy too. I needed empathy. The work on empathy wasn't just for others, it was also for me.

I soon discovered that working on empathy helped me. Instead of beating myself up for feeling afraid and stressed out, empathy helped me be kinder, more compassionate, and most important-ly, more patient with myself. With empathy, I could give myself the grace to feel and accept that the range of emotions I faced were natural under the circumstances.

How can empathy help you be kinder and more compassion-ate to yourself?

Inner Work Meets Outer Work

Just as focusing exclusively outward can be unhealthy when you fail to prioritize yourself, focusing solely inward can be unhealthy as well. You need to be able to toggle between the inner work and your own impact on the outer world.

In healing, you're working on the inner disconnections made between the parts of yourself, especially your heart. As you build kindness and compassion for self, the wisdom starts to naturally extend to others. You may find yourself looking at family members or friends differently. I call it "seeing others through the eyes of love."

Believe me, I didn't always see other people that way.

During my initial self-healing work, I'd picked up a book by Louise Hay called *You Can Heal Your Life*. The book was filled with useful information, powerful mantras, and beautiful meditations, but one specific line in the book caught my attention: "I forgive you for not being the way I wanted you to be."

WHAT?!

I repeated the words out loud a few times.
"I forgive you for not being the way **I** wanted you to be."
I emphasized the second "I." It was a swift awakening.

Did other people let me down? Or did I place expectations upon them and expect them to live up to them? I knew the answer.

It was extremely uncomfortable for me to consider the possibility that I had invented all the disappointments I felt toward others in my own head. *Am I a monster? How can I do that to people? Especially to the people I love most?*

But the truth was right there. I placed expectations, unrealistic ones, on others. I also expected them to read my mind and know what I expected of them, even if I didn't clearly express it to them in advance. And I was extremely comfortable expressing my disappointment when they didn't meet those expectations. Perhaps I was a monster, after all. *Oh, hello, Judger self.* It took me some time to reconcile this pattern of my behavior and forgive myself for it.

For me, the hardest part of working on empathy was realizing that the more deeply I loved someone, the more I expected them to live up to the image I'd set in my mind of who they should be.

My husband suffered the brunt of this more than anyone else.

One of the challenges of being a verbose individual is that I believed I had clearly communicated who I expected him to be, ALL THE TIME. We'd have these "deep conversations," which really meant I talked *at* him for an hour or two. After talking at him, I'd confirm that he'd heard me, then I'd wait for him to change. I expected him to immediately demonstrate a new behavior that met the expectations I'd placed upon him. When he failed to make any changes, my frustration intensified, and I'd interpret his inaction as proof that he didn't really love me. Because if he did, he would change. Right?

It is so hard to admit this, to write it down and share it with you.

Who can love someone who acts like this? My judger self loves it when I expose my weaknesses.

You are worthy of love, says my heart.

Thank you.

The inner work leads to the outer work. As I focused on *my* own expectations and not on the people I blamed for letting me down, I started to see other people in a new way. I started to see them without judging them.

I got more curious and asked more questions. What if my husband's actions were the way he showed me love? What if his intentions came from the best place possible? What if I could remember that what drove me crazy now was exactly what I fell in love with in the first place?

I toggled inward and outward. Why did I expect him to change? How did my expectations on him impact how he showed up in the world? How did it prevent him from growing in his own way? Seeing him in this light and holding space for him to just be who he is, without expectations, expanded my love for him.

Perhaps the most important revelation of all for me was why *I* was placing conditions on *him* and then measuring his ability to meet those expectations as proof of his level of love for me. That revelation changed everything.

Pay attention to your thoughts when you toggle outward. Think about the important people in your life. Do you lead with judgment or curiosity? Do you have a sense of knowing and certainty? If you do, you're likely making some assumptions, and often, the assumptions we make are wrong, or only partly right, which is still wrong.

Remember, empathy is about holding space for others, accepting them as they are, and sitting with them quietly without judgment.

Empathy and the World Around You

How do you embody empathy beyond those you love? How do you bring it to the rest of the world?

The more you focus on yourself and the expectations you may be placing upon others, the more curious you might get about what embodied empathy looks like in everyday interactions. I certainly wondered about that.

The idea of owning my part in the conflicts I had with others really spoke to me. I didn't need them to sort their stuff out, I needed to sort out what was mine. I wanted a way to release the other person from any responsibility to fix me.

Louise Hay's words kept playing in my head: "I forgive you for not being the way I wanted you to be." So, I started reciting the words as a daily forgiveness practice. Initially, I repeated the words three times in my head each day when I first woke up. This daily forgiveness practice set my intention of forgiving others throughout my day. It also helped me release any resentment or frustration I was feeling toward someone from the previous day.

As I noticed a change in my feelings, especially at home, I was curious to see where else a forgiveness practice could help me. I started reciting the same words in my head in the moment whenever I was with someone and felt irritated, be it at home, at work, on the subway—everywhere.

Saying these words in my head shifted my attention from the source of my frustration into a place of greater clarity, calm, and peace. That surprised me. How could one simple sentence shift me from frustration into peace? Somehow, it did.

I found that by practicing the forgiveness mantra each day, I connected more deeply with my heart, and empathy started to evolve from the work.

From this daily forgiveness practice, a new question formed in my mind: *What can I love about this person in this moment?*

On one particularly frustrating morning, I needed to take the subway to work. It had been a challenge getting the kids ready for school. Everyone was taking too long to get dressed, too long to eat breakfast, too long to brush their teeth, and way too long to get out the door. I was worked up, and I was running late. Ultimately, I missed the bus I needed to catch to get to work on time, which left me cursing under my breath.

By the time I reached the subway platform, it was packed with people.

Perfect! Just the way I love to travel on the subway. (My judger self tends to show up when I'm stressed out.) I tried to navigate the people and bags to get to my desired spot on the platform before the next train arrived.

As the train pulled into the station, I could see it was already full, and I knew that everyone on the platform was going to do their best to get on that train. Including me. The doors opened and we moved like cattle being corralled into a stall that wasn't big enough to hold us all. *Squish.* I removed my purse from my shoulder and placed it between my feet to make more room for the people around me.

A large backpack bumped me hard in the small of my back.

Ow!

Anger traveled from the spot on my back, up my spine, and toward my mouth that prepared to let the offender have it.

Forgiveness.

This one word moved quickly toward my mouth from my heart. I paused and took a deep breath.

I forgive you for not being the way I wanted you to be.

I recited the words of forgiveness in my head. The stab of pain in my lower back vanished and the anger was replaced with calm and peace.

Could that person have chosen to take off their backpack?

Yes.

Were they doing the best they could in this uncomfortable situation?

I chose to believe they were.

What can I love about this person in this moment?

I turned to glance briefly at the backpacked traveler and smiled at her. She breathed a sigh of relief and returned the smile. Instead of an angry exchange, our smiles sent us both off on our journeys for the day with more compassion and care. I knew that I would bring that positive energy with me. I expected that she would as well.

This exchange on the subway showed me something I hadn't noticed before: Our anger is contagious, and so is our forgiveness, compassion, and empathy.

For the next few weeks, whenever I traveled on the subway, I asked myself the same question: "What can I love about this person?" I looked at each person around me and instead of leading with judgment, I looked for one thing I loved about them. I noticed people's smiles, their shoes, their hairstyles, the way they spoke to the friends they were traveling with, the books they were reading . . . I found at least one thing I could love about each person on the train.

This practice made me aware of how quickly I typically judged other people solely on their appearance. And it also changed the way I wanted to love people just as they are, to see all people as beautiful souls doing the best they can with where they are at in that moment.

Whatever you choose to put out into the world spreads. How can you choose to put more love into the world? How can you show more empathy for others? What will happen if you do?

The Annual Fight

You might find it easier to forgive strangers than the people closest to you. You may be more easily triggered by the people you love, as you probably have higher expectations of them. You may place them on higher pedestals, thus giving them further to fall when they don't meet the expectations you've placed upon them.

When I worked in the corporate world, November was the busiest month of my year. In it, I ran a week of training, hosted a significant three-day event, then attended a four-day leadership conference in Florida. For three weeks straight, I was out every night, leaving the full parental responsibilities to my darling husband. This schedule occurred over five consecutive years.

Despite knowing and appreciating what a rock star Jason was during this challenging time each year, we'd have an annual fight. It occurred on the same day at the same time every year for five years. Imagine: five years!

The fight was predictable, and we both showed up the very same way to that fight every time: I'd come home on Saturday afternoon, pack a new bag, sleep in my own bed for one night, and head to the airport early for an 8 a.m. flight Sunday morning. At the front door, just before I left, the fight would occur.

"It must be nice to be going to Florida for four days," he'd say.

"You know this is a business trip. And after two weeks of being 'on,' hosting and engaging advisers at my own events, I get to sit in a frigidly cold meeting room for four days, engaging the leaders, and rarely enjoying the Florida weather at all. Yep, it's nice all right," I'd respond with sarcasm.

"You have no idea how hard it is single parenting for weeks on end while you're traveling for work," he'd reply.

It felt like he hadn't heard a word I'd said.

"Oh my god! Listen, my work affords us this lifestyle that *you* want to live. That work requires that I travel. You know that. If you want to change our lifestyle, I can change my job and be home more. It's up to you." With that, I'd walk out the door without expressing any love or offering a kiss goodbye.

We'd barely talk during the next four days I was away. While I missed him, I was so angry at him. How dare he blame me for working my ass off! I'm sure he shared the same feelings I had of not being heard or valued. But at that time, I didn't think at all about his feelings.

What I didn't understand then is that by simply changing how I show up in any interaction, I can change the whole experience for everyone. If I shift from judgment into empathy and compassion, I can change the entire conversation.

Imagine if I'd shown up with empathy and compassion during that annual fight. Even if he said the same words, how would the conversation be different? Consider this version:

"It must be nice to be going to Florida for four days," he'd say.

"You know, it is nice there. I wish you could come with me."

"You have no idea how hard it is single parenting for weeks on end while you're traveling for work," he'd reply.

"You're right. I don't. Maybe we can talk about that when I get back."

Without my expectations on him and my defensive, judgmental responses, there is no fight, just an opportunity to listen with love and show empathy for my husband's point of view. It would let him feel seen and heard. That's the recipe for deepening connections with those we love and inviting empathy for ourselves in the process.

Let's reflect.

This annual fight was a battle of the minds. What I heard him saying felt like scathing judgment, and it stung. So, I'd retaliate and sting right back.

But when I checked in with my heart, I discovered how I really felt. I had been wishing he could come on that trip with me. Going to Florida with him would have been a wonderful experience that I longed to have. Telling him that came from my heart.

When he'd say that he felt like a single parent, I heard judgment that I wasn't a good parent or a good wife. This sent my warrior self into battle mode. I felt like I was losing and needed to win, so I attacked him the same way I felt myself being attacked.

The truth is that at that time in our life, my husband never had days away from the kids. I really didn't know what that felt like, as I traveled for work all the time. He wasn't saying I was a bad parent or a bad partner—I knew that in my heart. What he was saying was that he was having a hard time. I heard it as criticism.

But the more I practiced shifting from judgment into empathy, the more I saw other people doing the best they could. And when I saw people doing the best they could, my heart opened further in an unexpected way: I began believing that people operated from a place of good intentions.

Something shifted within me, and I started to feel more joy more often. Believing that others act with good intentions brought me peace, and I loved feeling peace and joy.

What if seeing the best in others was the secret to feeling more peace and joy every day?

When I imagined our annual fight using the empathy I'd developed, I felt completely different toward my husband. I saw him doing the best he could. I saw his good intentions and his effort to share his truth with me. Old me just refused to listen and attacked him instead.

Living by heart helped me see things from his point of view. Empathy helped me look at that annual fight from a different perspective and really *see* the man standing in front of me, doing the best he could with where he was in that moment.

What would happen if you believed everyone tried to do their best? Not from a naive place but just believing in the best in others.

It's important to note that sometimes developing empathy for others hurts. My reflection on the annual fight with Jason revealed how I was showing up in the world. It showed me the impact I was having on him when I showed up in judgment.

Ouch!

I wasn't showing up as my best self in these moments, which led to a lot of internal judgment. Practicing empathy became important not only for those around me but for me too. I needed to build empathy for myself.

When you can't forgive yourself for your own flaws, it can be difficult to receive love from others. So having an empathy practice is for everyone, including you.

Empathy, Fear, and Grief

What are some things in your life you really worry about? What makes your thoughts spin? The better you understand what causes these thoughts, the more empathy you can bring to yourself and to others.

FEAR

Sometimes my thoughts can completely spin me into overwhelm. For example, at the start of 2020, my business was thriving, and my calendar was fully booked with workshops right through to the fall. My coaching clients were referring me to new clients and renewing their contracts, my corporate clients were calling looking for my availability, and I was celebrating.

Then COVID happened. In February, corporate clients called to postpone workshops, and by March, they had canceled them completely. My coaching clients asked if they could defer their calls until the chaos at work settled down, and my once-full calendar looked empty.

I started to panic. I worried whether my business would survive. What would happen to me? What would happen to my family? I imagined losing our house. I imagined all the worse-case scenarios.

I knew I needed some tools to help me manage the fears causing my mind to spin. Breathing, with one hand on my heart and one hand on my gut, was one tool I used often during those early weeks of fear. Breathing helped me get centered and focused. It helped me shift from doomsday thinking into my inner wisdom, recognizing that I can navigate challenging times and creatively solve problems.

I started putting my energy and love into action. "Living by Heart" became a daily series of live videos on Facebook. I showed up every day sharing the practices I was using to navigate the stress and fear of being trapped at home for an indefinite period.

But the biggest difference I experienced during this time of stress and fear was the empathy I had for myself. Instead of judging myself for my fear, I could give myself grace and accept that my fear was natural.

When I checked in with my heart, I knew that my corporate clients weren't canceling because they didn't want me to facilitate for them. They were canceling because they, too, were navigating the unknown. My coaching clients weren't deferring their coaching sessions because they didn't want to work with me; they couldn't focus on their growth while trying to manage their team and their clients' fears.

Empathy helped me see others doing the best they could where they were at in that moment. Empathy helped me see that I was doing the best I could. This same practice was enormously helpful at home too.

My home, which had been my private, peaceful office during the day for three years, was suddenly filled full-time with four other people. Four other people trying to work and go to school at home for the very first time. Four other people trying to find their own space and privacy, trying to create new routines, and trying to manage their own stress and fears. I'm so grateful I'd already started my empathy work before COVID.

I needed all the empathy I'd learned to show up for Jason and the kids the way I wanted to be for them. To support the boys in their frustration over online school and lots of confusion each day. To support Jason as we both found ways to give each other space and privacy, and to find ways to laugh in the face of what seemed so absurd.

How can empathy help you navigate your fears? What could grace and acceptance bring you when you judge yourself? Take a few moments now to reflect on the fears you identified and how empathy can help you shift from spinning to grace and acceptance. If it helps, put one hand on your heart and the other on your gut as you reflect. Take a few deep cleansing breaths. Imagine that on the in-breath you're taking in fresh, clean air, and on the out-breath you're releasing any tension or stress you may be holding.

This is a grounding activity you can do anywhere whenever you want to get focused and connected with your heart and your gut. Connecting with your heart and your gut helps you be who you want to be in your life and in your work.

(You'll find more tips in "Empathy as a Practice" at the end of the Empathy section.)

GRIEF

Grief is part of life. When you love others, you know that grief comes with love. How you grieve and how you give yourself space to grieve takes empathy. Being with and supporting others when they grieve also takes empathy.

We used to have Sunday dinners at my mom's house a few times a month. After years of gently trying to encourage Mom to move into a retirement residence, she'd made the decision to move in the fall of 2019. It took us a few months of searching for the right place together before my mom chose to move to a residence in Richmond Hill, a neighborhood not too far from midtown Toronto.

Mom decided to move in first and make sure she liked living there before she sold her house. This seemed like a reasonable decision at the time. She moved into her new apartment at the residence on February 1, 2020, and six weeks later found herself in lockdown due to the pandemic.

We weren't allowed to visit her, and she wasn't allowed to leave. With a house to clear and sell, Mom and I would need empathy to work together on the challenges that faced us.

At this time, Jason's parents had been hosting us for dinner on Tuesday nights for almost a decade. It was a special night each week that the boys looked forward to. They loved spending time with Nana and Pa. Nana had been diagnosed with ovarian cancer in 2017, and while her treatment had kept the cancer from spreading, COVID put her at high risk, and our weekly dinners needed to be put on hold. Distanced backyard visits with masks became an option a few months into the pandemic, but we all grieved the loss of joy we'd had during those weekly dinners.

Empathy helped us navigate the initial grief we experienced from the distance and reduced in-person time with loved ones we cared so much about, and the distance prevented us from seeing the decline in the health of both of our mothers.

Jason's mom passed away in July 2021. Jason had been by her side for four days straight while she was in the hospital, sleeping on the floor beside her and keeping her spirits up when she was awake. After a few close calls, she seemed to stabilize on the fourth day, so Jason came home for the night to sleep in his own bed. His mom passed away in the early morning hours while he slept at home.

Empathy played a vital role in the days and weeks that followed as we supported each other, the boys, and Pa through the grieving process. Then, just weeks after Jason's mom died, my mom was diagnosed with the very same cancer. It was stage four and there was little that could be done for Mom aside from keeping her comfortable.

Jason, in the throes of grief over the loss of his mom, bravely spoke his truth. He wanted to give me everything I needed, but he had little capacity to support me. I'm so grateful for empathy. I could see him, love him, and appreciate that he was doing the best he could with where he was at during that time. This helped us both navigate our grief together and independently.

Building an empathy practice helped me access my empathy when I was under immense stress, facing intense fears, and navigating unimaginable grief.

Having a daily empathy practice supports you when times get tough. It's like a muscle that you exercise regularly so when you start the race you don't need to think about moving your muscles, they just move from memory. Visit "Empathy as a Practice" for tips on how to grow daily practices.

Mom's Last Visit with the Boys

Empathy helps you navigate the hard stuff. When you can see people through the eyes of love, believe that they're doing the best they can, and trust that they're acting with the best of intentions, you can show up as the person you want to be with them. Living by heart lets you lead with empathy every day.

On March 18, 2022, the final day of March Break, I insisted that the boys come with me to visit Grandma. Two of my three teenage sons grudgingly came with me. When we arrived, Mom seemed more uncomfortable than usual. She grinned through clenched teeth, and I could tell she was happy to see the boys. They sat down near her and jumped right into stories about what they were up to. Mom listened intently and the pain she was experiencing seemed a distant memory.

Thirty minutes into our visit, the nurse came to check on Mom. They didn't like the color of her skin or the pain she told them she was experiencing. The nurse called Mom's doctor. He advised Mom to go to the hospital. He would meet her there.

The nurse called for an ambulance. The boys stood awkwardly as the paramedics loaded Grandma on the stretcher and wheeled her out of the room. I told Mom I'd meet her at the hospital after driving the boys home. She smiled at them and waved as she rolled away. I didn't know it would be the last time they would see her.

No one spoke a word on the drive home.

I felt my eyes welling with tears. *Hold it together*, I demanded silently to myself.

Gently, said my heart. *Being upset is human.*

I worried that I'd scare the boys if I cried. They'd been through enough, having lost their paternal grandmother just seven months earlier.

On my way back to the hospital, the tears flowed openly. I considered pulling over to wait for the floodgates to pass but reconsidered because there was no real end in sight.

I considered putting on some music, but I knew anything I played would only make me miss Mom more.

Christ, Heather! She's still here, the old familiar voice of my judger self said, chiming in with criticism.

Gently, love, my heart answered. *There are no rules for grief. It comes when it comes.*

I felt a gentle breeze of compassion blowing over me. My breathing slowed down, and my stomach started to settle. By the time I got to the emergency room at the hospital, I had anchored into love and compassion for Mom. That was the version of me that she needed. And I did too.

How can empathy and connecting with your heart support you during times of grief? What insights can you take from this story to apply to your own experiences? Paying attention to your emotions, connecting with your heart, and choosing empathy can help you shift during challenging times so you can show up the way you want to.

The Gifts of 2022

When you do the work, you receive gifts beyond imagination. There are likely a few obvious things you can see in your life that could be improved with some empathy. Others may surprise you like a gift you receive on your birthday that you didn't ask for.

From empathy, I received three gifts in 2022: presence, compassion, and grace.

The gift of **presence**. I'm grateful for the time I got to spend with Mom during her final months of life. Being present for her, with her, was a gift I could choose to give us both. I'm grateful for the empathy my heart let me give myself so I could ask my clients to reschedule instead of listening to my judger self who called me selfish and told me no one would think it was reasonable to take time off. I'm grateful for my caring clients whose understanding allowed me to shift my schedule and prioritize what really mattered.

The gift of **compassion**. Compassion was my theme word entering 2022, as I knew I was going to need it for the months ahead with Mom. As her health declined, compassion helped me show up every day with love for her. I wanted to be sure she felt loved, supported, and safe no matter what. It was challenging at times, but my work on empathy helped me continue to love her where she was at on her journey. What I learned from leading with compassion and heart with Mom, I was also able to extend to my dad, my sister, Jason, the kids, and myself.

The gift of **grace**. I mistakenly thought that in grieving for Mom while she was sick, I wouldn't need time to grieve when she died. Oh man, was I ever wrong! I was shocked by the grief I felt when Mom was finally freed from the body that had cruelly failed her. I didn't expect I'd need so much time and space. Initially, I struggled with guilt over it. *Why wasn't I stronger? More resilient? Better able to cope?*

Then, through empathy, I found grace and let myself breathe in the space I needed to heal. Grace might be the greatest gift of all.

Grace helped me release from all the "shoulds" my judger self placed upon me in 2022.

I should be working harder.

I should be marketing more.

I should be putting myself out there (whatever that means).

I should have more clients.

I should be making more money.

I should be eating better.

I should be exercising more.

I should take that course.

I should turn off Netflix, Disney+ . . .

I really should get up and shower.

But even a shower, on certain days, felt like too much. Embracing grace helped me shift from the "shoulds" and allowed me to "be" exactly who I needed to be in the moment. Grace lifted the terrible weight of "should." Without the daily empathy practice I'd built, I doubt I would've discovered grace.

What gifts might you receive from developing your own empathy practice? How might empathy help you be more present, more compassionate toward others, or help you find grace for yourself?

Empathy as a Practice

What are the steps for building your empathy practice?

Like in Healing, you can learn about yourself and your own empathy through a reflective practice.

My preferred method of reflection is journaling. If you haven't journaled before or know that journaling is a good medium for you, here are the steps I take each day in my empathy practice. You may wish to start with one of these activities, then choose to build your own practice over time.

SETTING INTENTIONS:

In the morning, I take a few moments to write and set my intentions for living with empathy that day.

Today, I embody empathy for those I love.
Today, I look for the best in others.
Today, I lead with love and compassion.

Explore what words work best for you. You don't need to use the exact words I use. In fact, it can be more effective if you find your own words that ground you and feel like who you want to be when you're interacting with others.

IN THE MOMENT:

Throughout the day, I practice forgiveness when I feel myself sitting in judgment. It helps me shift into empathy and compassion. You'll remember Louise Hay's words:

"I forgive you for not being the way I wanted you to be."

The other phrase I recite in my head throughout the day is "lead with love."

This quick three-word phrase can help me shift when I am with Jason, or my kids, and I feel my warrior self getting ready to battle.

"Lead with love, lead with love, lead with love."

It brings down the temperature in my body, slows the speed of my mind, and shifts me from judgment into compassion for the person in front of me.

END OF DAY REFLECTION:

At the end of the day, I reflect in my journal, or alternatively, I ask myself these questions as I prepare for sleep.

1. How did I embody empathy today?
2. Where could I be more caring and compassionate?
3. What do I want to work on tomorrow?

If you notice some judgment when you ask yourself reflective questions, that's normal, especially in the beginning. You can thank your judger self, then take a moment to connect with your heart. If helpful, place one hand on your heart and take a few slow, cleansing breaths. Imagine you're breathing in love and compassion. Then breathe out and let go of judgment and criticism.

OTHER WAYS TO BUILD EMPATHY:

You can work on building your empathy during self-guided or guided meditation, yoga, or other guided activities like Reiki, EFT (discussed in Healing), and breathwork (discussed in Awareness and Resilience). I encourage you to explore what works best for you. You may choose to work with a coach on building empathy too. When working with a coach, you might design your own framework to explore empathy for yourself and for others.

During one coaching session with my own coach, for example, we created a framework that allows me to check in on what I want compassion and kindness for myself to look like in a particular moment.

The framework starts with the question: What does kindness/compassion for me look like right now?

Most recently, I answered this question with:

Kindness for me looks like being . . .

Kind when I eat
Kind when I drink
Kind to my body
Kind in my current state, when there's a lot going on.

Take a moment to ask yourself this question: "What does kindness or compassion for myself look like right now?" If it helps, place one hand on your heart as you check in with yourself. Write down your answers in your journal or another notebook.

As you read your own answers, what do you notice? If this is the first time you've asked yourself what kindness to yourself looks like, it might feel a little strange or uncomfortable. Notice if your judger self is getting in the way. This activity isn't selfish. Learning how to be kind to yourself helps you be kind to others.

The second question in the framework is: What kind of kindness do I want to choose for myself?

If you aren't sure what kindness means to you, there are a series of questions to connect with the parts of yourself:

What does kindness look like?
What does kindness feel like?
What does kindness smell like?
What does kindness taste like?

Painting a clear picture of the compassion and kindness you want to have toward yourself helps you live outwardly with empathy, kindness, and compassion toward others. If your own tank is drained, you can't show up the way you want to with the people around you.

AWARENESS

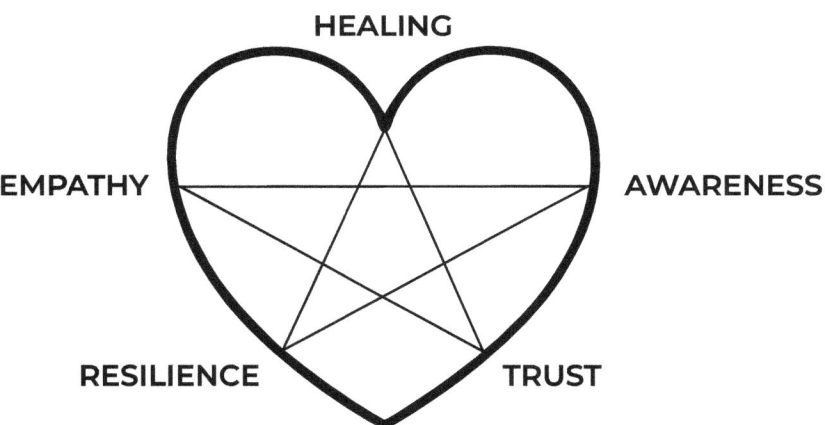

HEALING

EMPATHY

AWARENESS

RESILIENCE

TRUST

What Is Awareness?

If you want to build your personal brand, design the *you* you want to be and way you want people to feel when they're with you, you start with awareness. After healing, it's the foundation of the work you do on yourself. Without awareness, you cannot see the systems you operate in, the role you play, and the changes you may want to make within the systems and within yourself.

Awareness connects you with all your parts. Awareness is like a sound board that lets you turn up the dial so you can hear the muted parts of yourself and turn down the volume on the loud ones. Adjusting the dial also helps you notice any silent parts you may have. Awareness lets you step outside yourself so you can observe what's happening within you. Awareness lets you question and challenge your own perceived reality.

Without awareness, we'd all be walking around convinced that what we see is fact and there is no other way. Thank goodness for awareness!

In the Introduction, I talked about Parts Work and discovering the various parts of myself. I introduced you to my Itty Bitty Sh*tty Committee, the IBSC, and the parts of myself that like to get in my way. I know those parts think they're helping me and are worthy of love. But man, they can really throw me off course! The warrior self, judger self, and comparison self are just a few of the members I've talked about so far from my IBSC.

After I finished my coaching certification, I thought I'd done all the awareness work I could ever need. I thought I'd nipped that dissonant IBSC choir in the proverbial vocal cords and silenced them all for good. *Good riddance!* But my warrior self was just quietly rebuilding her army and gathering reinforcements.

The hardest part of working on yourself may be the realization and acceptance that the work is never truly finished. *Yep, you're a mess. You'll always be a work in progress.* Thank you, Judger self.

My heart knows this work also brings the greatest joy. It asks, *What would you do if the journey was already over?*

Awareness still manages to surprise me. I continue to discover new things about myself every day, and my mind can get exhausted by it. The more work I do, the more I discover. The more I discover, the more work I must do. Then my heart reminds me that life is a journey, not a destination, so have fun and enjoy the ride.

Awareness, like healing and empathy, is a practice. Through practice you can prepare for challenges ahead, stay present in the moment, and reflect after on what you've learned. There's a process to awareness: taking action, reflecting on the action, and learning from the action, as you'll see in the stories I share about awareness. You'll also have the opportunity to reflect on the parts of yourself as well as the learning you want to take with you.

The more you learn about yourself, the more empowered you are. The more empowered you are, the more you can evolve and shine your own light brightly.

The Ego: Self as Parent

You don't have to be a parent to imagine it as a difficult job. Parents carry the responsibility of raising another human while also shouldering the responsibility for raising and managing themselves. It's no small feat.

If you're a seasoned parent, congratulations—you've survived! If you're a new parent, congratulations (and don't worry, you'll survive)! If you aren't a parent, I invite you to connect with the role in the family system with which you're most familiar: whether you're an aunt, uncle, cousin, daughter, son, niece, or nephew, know you play a part in the system. And how you show up in that system impacts all members of it, including you.

Jason and I have three sons, and while we have been on the parenting journey for over twenty years now, I've learned more about myself as parent in the last two years than I learned in the previous eighteen. That's saying something.

It's been a challenge for sure, and I've literally wanted to quit many times. I've wanted to run for the hills or move to another country. The thing is, as a parent, you can't quit. Even if you want to.

Friends and I joke about it—this "parenting thing" we signed up for without any real idea of just how hard it was truly going to be. As a control freak, when I realized that all semblance of control was just a mirage . . . well, it's hard not to jump in the car and drive as far away as I possibly can to free myself from this gig I agreed to do. *What was I thinking?!*

No matter how many parenting books you read, how much advice you take, or how many careful plans you make, parenting teenagers is like running a marathon with an ever-changing obstacle course you can't train for in advance. Oh, and add in a roller-coaster ride, just for fun.

My journey into living by heart began when my boys were still quite small, and I still believed the illusion that I had control. In those days, my greatest struggles were getting the boys to bathe, go to bed on time, get dressed for school, and get out the door.

Despite how small those daily activities look in the bigger picture today, each battle felt like an insurmountable barrier in that moment. My go-to response in those early parenting days when I couldn't control things was unleashing anger.

One quiet evening years ago when the kids were finally asleep, Jason and I watched a movie called *Playing by Heart*. It's a character film about family dynamics and the complexity of love, loss, trust, and fear. Whenever a character appeared to get irrationally angry, the others called them "Anger ball." We loved the term so much that we started using it in our relationship. It served as a reminder that when things got heated, perhaps we were being irrational, and just saying the term "anger ball" brought some levity to the moment. We'd usually end up laughing.

No matter how many times people would say not to stress the small things, I struggled with the little things I couldn't control at home. Often, my "anger ball" rage delicately teetered below the surface of the smiling veneer I tried desperately to maintain.

As I started to understand what living by heart could look and feel like at home, the role my ego played in these power-struggle interactions came into clear view. Ugh.

My ego made meaning of every challenging moment.

Why won't he just get dressed?
I must be a bad mom.
He doesn't love me. If he did, he would do what I say.
Why won't he just let me put his seatbelt on?
He's trying to make me late.
Why will he put his coat on at school and not at home?
He must respect his teacher more than me.
He's testing me to see who will give in first.

Seriously, these were the thoughts I had about my three-year old. *Hello, Judger self.* My inner dialogue was vicious and relentless. The more my son resisted putting on his coat, the more determined I was to prove that I could "make" him put it on.

It reminds me of Karpman's drama triangle that I frequently reference in my coaching work with clients when they're experiencing conflict in their lives.

I see the drama and the roles I played in it. I'd swiftly move from one position to another, always trying to control the outcome.

First, my son was in the victim position, and I tried to "rescue" him from the trouble he was having putting on his coat.

Then, when that didn't work, I shifted into persecutor: "Why don't you have your coat on yet?! Hurry up!" I'd demand, while additional thoughts directed at my son spun in my head: *What's wrong with you? Can't you do anything right?*

And finally, when that didn't work, I shifted to the victim position, pointing out what my three-year-old son was "doing" to me.

I am not sure which position bribing falls under, but I sometimes resorted to that too.

While I didn't know what else to do back then, I did know that I wasn't being the mom I wanted to be. My judger self and the rest of the IBSC loved it when I felt bad about my parenting.

You're a sh*tty mom.
How could you judge your kid like that? Who does that?
Everyone else can get their kids to school on time, so what's wrong with you?

This inner assault only made me feel worse, angrier, and even less in control.

With compassion, I can now see myself stuck in patterns that didn't serve my son or me in the moment. Yet, I was doing the best I could for where I was at during that time. I couldn't tell that my ego was driving my behavior and not my heart.

As I spent more time doing inner work, I began understanding the role my ego was playing. I started seeing my ego outside myself. I could sense her and notice when she was feeling stepped on or offended in some way.

As I started getting curious about her, I even started feeling some love for her. As a part of myself, I could see how my ego helped me achieve a lot of success in my life. Her ambition, her bravery, her relentless determination—these were all positive traits of my ego. I needed her. I also needed to understand when her domineering style wasn't helping me, others, or the situation.

I can see how my ego has played a part in writing this book. The awareness work continues!

You might ask, "How long does it take to write a book?" Well, there are obvious elements such as creating the structure, brain-storming the content, and the time it takes to write the words on the page. Then there's editing, post-production, and publishing.

What you may not know is what happens before that. Writing a book begins long before a single word is written. It starts as an idea percolating in your mind. I started thinking about this book back in 2012 when my living by heart journey began. So, why did it take me so long to write it?

Fear.

My ego hijacked my plans first by asking, *Who am I to write a book? Who wants to read what I have to say?*

My judger self replied, *No one.*

Thank you, Judger self.

One of my favorite definitions of fear is **f**alse **e**vidence **a**ppearing **r**eal. My ego, judger self, and the rest of the IBSC worked hard to create stories that kept me from writing this book. For years, even though I was living by heart, the book was only an idea. I didn't realize I was my own worst enemy, letting my IBSC get in the way of sharing my experiences with others in the book I dreamed about.

My ego didn't silence me completely, though. In the early days of my journey, my heart was battling my ego, and when my heart won briefly, I wrote posts about my experiences on Facebook. When I posted about living by heart, people responded positively, and some would ask me, "When are you going to write a book?"

Even with their encouragement, support, and love, I was too scared to get started.

As I mentioned earlier, I started a daily live video series on Facebook during the COVID pandemic called "Living by Heart" where I shared some of the ideas included in this book. But while putting myself out there on camera each day did increase my confidence and tell me there was increasing interest in this topic, I was still too afraid to write this book.

After all the self-work I'd done, what was still getting in the way? Yes, fear. But what was this fear all about?

After a lot of work on healing my inner wounds and building love for myself, after a lot of work building empathy and living with compassion for others, I still needed to work on my ego. I'm grateful that I did so much healing and empathy work first because I was going to need it when I dove into awareness and understanding my ego.

As you explore your own ego and deepen your own awareness of the various parts of yourself, you may want to return to Healing or Empathy to support you. The journey to living by heart isn't a straight line, and if you feel drawn to return to earlier parts of this book, do so without judgment. Connect with your heart to stay open, curious, and kind to yourself.

The Ego: Observing Your Ego

Have you ever had an "out of ego" experience? A moment when your consciousness steps out of your body and stands over it, witnessing what's happening within you? It feels a bit like the first time the Ancient One knocks the consciousness out of Dr. Strange's body in Marvel's *Dr. Strange*. Tilda Swinton, who played the Ancient One, takes one hand and with one swift push separates Benedict Cumberbatch, who played Dr. Strange, from his body. Woosh!

The first time I had an "out of ego" experience, we were driving to Niagara-on-the-Lake.

Jason's mom ran a clothing store on the main street in this quaint Ontario town, and it's a beautiful place to spend a Saturday afternoon. The drive was stressful and long, however, especially with three young boys. We were fortunate that they were experienced and easy-going travelers.

To ease the time, we listened to a playlist of songs we all enjoyed. Midway through our journey, a great song by Sarah Harmer, "Uniform Grey," played, and Jason and I both smiled.

"I love this song," I said. "Remember when we had the camp gang over and Ellen's sister sang this song?"

"Yeah," said Jason. "She had an amazing voice!"

The car suddenly got very quiet, even with Sarah's melodic voice playing in the background. Fear on Jason's face appeared, and he looked straight ahead.

My mind raced.

What does he mean? Does he think she sings better than me? Does he think I'm a bad singer?

It was at this point that I had my first "out of ego" experience. I separated from those thoughts and could see them as if they stood before me. It felt like time had stopped as I witnessed what was happening within myself.

How did I get here? What had been the words he'd actually said? "She had an amazing voice."

And what did I hear? *She sings better than you do.*

How fascinating!

I could see my ego twisting Jason's words into some kind of attack on me. He hadn't said anything about me, he'd just acknowledged another human having an amazing voice. And even I had to admit that what he said was true. She did have an amazing voice. Yet I could see him worried that he'd set himself up for an attack, and he'd put on his armor. He was ready for it.

Man, was I that predictable? How often did I overreact? How often was I triggered by innocent, well-intentioned comments that I then turned into something else? It was obvious I did it often, as his reaction was a trained response.

I took a deep breath. Jason held his.

"You know," I said, "I have serious ego issues."

Jason let out a sigh of relief and his face showed his surprise.

"Serious ego issues," I repeated and laughed.

Then he laughed too. We laughed together as I shared with him my whole thought process and what I'd just observed within myself.

The battle Jason had been bracing for was averted. For the first time, I saw how my ego set me up for more conflict in my life than I really faced in the world. I saw just how manipulative and deceiving my ego could be. How quick I was to anger and overreact. How easily my ego twisted what was said into something I could be angry about. I'd have to practice having "out of ego" experiences more often.

This was the start of a new relationship with my ego, of living by heart consciously in my relationships.

Give yourself time now to reflect. Where is your ego standing in your way? Is there a specific relationship or situation where you notice your ego is present? Or perhaps this example has raised some curiosity for you to explore how your ego shows up in interactions with others.

Consider how you might step out of your body when your ego takes over, witness it, and choose to change your reaction as a result.

If you're not used to observing or noticing your ego in action, the tell-tale sign she's in control is when unexpected emotions surface. Often quickly. A sudden burst of emotion is a good indicator it's time to pause, step away, and unpack the inner dialogue that the ego is trying to urge you to react to.

The practice of bringing my ego into awareness has served me well over the years. I've used it many times, both personally and professionally, to slow down, pause, and choose an action instead of reaction.

The Ego: Anger Ball and Peaches

So, now that we've looked at the ego and the way she manipulates information, making her own meaning regardless of the facts, let's bring her into consciousness in other relationships.

This would be a good time for you to make a list. Which people in your life currently, or in the past, set you off? Not everyone has the fight response of the warrior self, so you may recognize an avoider self, quiet self, or even the tuned-out self as possible responses to the ego making meaning of an interaction. Some people call this "getting triggered."

Once you have your list, you can replay an event with your heart present. First, send your ego and your judger self outside to play on the swings together. If it helps you, put your hand on your heart to stay connected as you replay the event.

What was said? How did you hear it? Do the two stories align?

What was your inner dialogue saying to you about that event? Is there anything you can see now that you didn't see then? What would you do differently if you could do it over?

On the top of my list, after Jason, came my kids. There are so many moments when my kids were small that I would do over if I could. Everything felt like a battle in those days, and I took it all personally. Whether one son refused to put on his shoes, or another refused to wear his coat, I unknowingly made it about me, and my temper would respond with lightning-bolt precision. You hurt me, I hurt you.

My warrior self's weapon of choice has always been my voice. I could cut the strongest warrior with my scathing tongue, which knew just where to strike to leave the deepest wound. I'd love to tell you that my children, the deepest loves in my heart, were spared the brunt of my warrior's rage, but in the early years, that wasn't always true.

I did try to manage the beast. I tried to contain her wrath. And most times, I was quite good at keeping her sword sheathed. But when I was tired and overheating in my winter coat, and my patience was stretched to the limit, she'd escape my clutches and lash out.

"If you don't put your coat on by the count of three, there will be serious consequences." I know now that these raging, yet idle, threats held no real weight. I hadn't decided what the consequences would be, and the kids knew I would forget by the time we got home that night.

I didn't know why I raged. At that time, I hadn't done much inner work to understand myself and why things set me off the way they did. What I did have, though, was an awareness that I didn't like who I was when the warrior took over. I didn't want to parent that way. I didn't want to live that way.

As I reflected on my latest poor parenting moment, I remembered the term "anger ball." Yes, I was being an anger ball. Now, what was I going to do about it?

The universe answered. That very same day, I happened to read an article about a mom who had committed to 365 days without yelling. She'd written a blog about her journey. I felt both excited and nervous. *Can I meet this challenge? What if I fail?*

Still, I couldn't stop thinking about it. A few days later, I decided to try it for myself. I needed to set some ground rules and get some support. I told the kids that I was going to commit to not yelling for a year. I was terrified that I'd fail, and the kids were skeptical too.

I asked them if they'd be willing to help, and they seemed excited by the invitation.

"Great! What word could we use to help Mommy not yell?" I asked them. They seemed unsure.

"What if there was one word you could say to me that let me know I was starting to yell before it happened?" I asked, prompting them. "What would that one word be?"

That seemed clearer to them, and they started thinking. After a few minutes, one of my darling boys looked up at me with wide-eyed wonder. "What about 'peaches,' Mommy?"

I laughed. Yes, peaches would do. It was light and fun, and I felt myself instantly shift when I heard his sweet voice say that one word.

We were ready, and I started the challenge. I would attempt 365 days without yelling.

The first few days went well. *This is easy,* I thought.

Then I had a week-long business trip. *Easy-peasy. I don't know what I was sweating about. I can do this.*

When I came home from my trip, I had a few sleepless nights and some added work stress. The patience that had come so easily started waning. Then one morning, we fell into that old familiar routine where everything was a battle. I couldn't find my composure and before I knew it, my warrior self surfaced and started to raise her blade.

That darling little face with the wide eyes looked scared. My son took a deep breath and touched my arm. "Peaches, Mommy."

My armor crumbled; my sword dropped. I knelt and wrapped him in a warm embrace. "Thank you," I said as I looked into those deep brown eyes. His fear was gone and only love remained.

This happened before I knew my heart would lead my crusade into kindness.

I didn't make the connection between my heart and the softness of the calm, patient, compassionate mother I wanted to be. All I knew then was my need to tame the warrior within me. And one simple word, peaches, was all it took to leave my "anger ball" behind.

As you reflect on this story, how does it relate to the relationships on your list? How could asking for help from others support you? Is there a word or phrase that could help you shift from judgment and reaction into the calm, compassionate self you want to be?

In the next section on resilience, we'll talk about how important self-care is for living by heart. When you're tired, stressed, or overwhelmed, it is so much harder to connect with and listen to your heart. Heck, even if you're hangry—hungry and angry—it's hard to listen to your heart.

Finding strategies that work for you and engaging those you care about most to support you can truly make all the difference. Peaches, love.

The Ego: Anger, Fire, and Kuan Yin

Emotions can catch you by surprise. You know the people who regularly rile you up, but every now and then someone you normally get along with says something that sets your ego into overdrive. This is when having a daily awareness practice and focusing on catching and taming the ego can really help—when the unexpected happens.

The following story captures a moment when my ego caught me by surprise, then awareness, along with some support from the universe, brought me back and connected me with my heart.

In 2019, long before writing this book, I was building a program for whole-self living. Working with a brand coach, I developed the vision for my ideal client along with the program content. The next step was creating a free offer to share with my target market. My brand coach provided me with the three-part, free-offer template, and I started building out my offer. It didn't come easily.

After weeks of struggle and spinning, I finally found myself in the creative zone. The words flowed from me as if they were coming straight from my soul. I crafted all three of my video scripts in just a few short hours. I was happy and felt complete.

On a bright, brisk November morning, I traveled to the location where we'd be shooting the videos. When I arrived, my brand coach and her makeup artist greeted me. We ate some delicious snacks and drank coffee, then the makeup artist asked me about my desired "look" for the shoot and proceeded to work her magic. As she finished the final touch, a pair of gorgeous fake lashes, my coach brought out her oracle cards—a beautiful set of Goddess Power cards, each holding their own wisdom. She invited me to draw a card for the video session.

I shuffled the deck slowly, feeling each card as they passed through my fingers. Electricity surged between the cards and my hands. I could feel the energy of the universe as I shuffled the two halves of the deck together. I listened for my message to stop and select a card. When the message arrived, I chuckled as I held the card chosen just for me in my hand. Hecate—"the In-between"—dazzled before me. *Of course. This makes perfect sense. I've been caught in the in-between for some time.*

You see, I often felt that my transformation was incomplete, that I only partially embraced my spiritual side. My ego had been telling me that my clientele wouldn't connect or appreciate my spiritual self, so I had to keep it hidden. I was half in and half out on my journey.

As I looked closely at the beautiful Hecate card, a second card fell from the deck. Curious. Clearly my guides had another message for me. I picked it up from the chair it landed on and turned it over. Kuan Yin—"Compassion"—looked up at me from the card. I felt her eyes on me. I felt her warmth.

Unlike with Hecate, I didn't really understand the meaning of Kuan Yin's appearance that morning. I loved the beauty of her card, though, so I treasured it without really knowing her purpose for the day ahead.

My brand coach placed the two cards on the table. They were propped up so I could see them from the chair I'd sit in during my video shoot. My coach then invited me to join her on the floor so we could discuss my scripts and create some supportive cue cards.

Excited, I pulled out my script and walked her through the three videos. They outlined the essence of the soul work I was doing. The signature program we'd worked on for months was captured in three brief vignettes of heart, gut, and body. It felt great to share them with her.

I noticed almost immediately her look of awe, which then shifted to something like confusion. She started to shake her head. What was up? I felt my heart rate increase. It thumped in my chest. Something was wrong. A new energy started coursing through me. I could feel the temperature on my skin rise.

"This won't work," she said.

I could feel my blood starting to boil. *What do you mean, this won't work?*

My lips didn't move. I didn't move. *I worked on this for hours. It is exactly what I want.* Still, I remained silent.

"The videos aren't supposed to be your signature program. This is a separate offering," I heard her say with a matter-of-fact tone that set my "anger ball" rage ablaze. *Hello, Warrior self.*

I could no longer hear her. What I heard instead were the raging thoughts in my own head.

Not good enough.
You're so stupid.
What a waste of time.

Oh, hello, Judger self.

I didn't know who I was angrier with, her or myself. I directed my rage at her, though. As my stare shifted to a glare, I felt this strong urge to get up and walk out.

I'm done. This is the end of our work together.

My thoughts raced, my mind raged, and all I could see was red. Fire. I still didn't move.

It felt like an eternity with the two of us sitting there in silence. I knew she could feel my rage. It was palpable. After some time, she broke the silence with an invitation to ask for divine guidance. "Let's meditate on it together," she offered. "Let's ask the Divine for guidance and see what we're directed to do."

Still raging inside, I remained silent. *You can. I am just going to sit here and fume.*

But as she began to call on the Divine, the mothers and fathers of all religions, I closed my eyes. Deep breath in. Red. Red. Red. Deep breath out. Rage. Rage. Rage. Deep breath in . . .

Suddenly I felt a sense of peace and calm wash over me. I saw the image of Kuan Yin, the Divine Goddess of Compassion. I felt her join me to offer her guidance.

Love her where she's at, the voice said.
Love yourself where you're at, the voice said, continuing.
See this through the eyes of compassion.
Yes, my love, said my heart in response.

Red turned to brilliant white light. The rage gone, now replaced with peace and calm.

See this through the eyes of compassion. I heard the words in my head again.

When I opened my eyes, the room felt completely different. I saw my brand coach through a new lens and could see her concern, her love, her true care for me and the situation. I could see what responsibility she was carrying, all things I couldn't see when I'd been overcome with wild "anger ball" rage.

I spoke out loud for the first time. "I'm open to whatever you recommend. How do you suggest we proceed?" I asked. The words felt as though they came through me rather than from me. I didn't recognize my own voice. Could I be staying and receiving instead of fighting or fleeing?

She looked as shocked as I felt. And then a little relieved.

"I thought you were going to walk out," she said.

"So did I," I said candidly. "I almost did." I breathed in a breath of fresh air as if clearing any remaining negative energy within me. She took a long, deep breath too.

"I think we should clear the negative energy in the room," she suggested as she stood up. "Let's clear each other."

A lighter sat on the table right in front of the two Goddess Power cards. She lit some palo santo and cleared my energy first. When she was done, I took the smoking stick and proceeded to clear her of any remaining negative energy from the conflict between us.

She reached for the lighter once more to relight the incense and clear the room. She yelped and jumped back. The lighter was still ablaze on the table. She grabbed it again, this time from the bottom, and held it up. We both gasped as we looked at this lighter, burning freely on its own. The lighter was raging. She moved quickly to the sink to put out the flame and run cold water on her burned hand.

I've never seen a lighter do that before. As my coach stood at the sink, I noticed the Hecate card had fallen over and the lighter had burned the left half of it. *The past,* I heard a voice within me say. I was no longer stuck in the "in-between."

Kuan Yin stood on the table looking knowingly at me. *Yes,* she said. *And compassion is your future.* The long-standing warrior within had received permission to rest. I felt another wash of peace flow over me. And with it, gratitude—gratitude for the gift of that moment; gratitude for the conflict and the invitation to choose a different path. The path of compassion.

My brand coach returned from the kitchen, and we embraced. I asked what she thought of the lighter igniting. She confirmed what I believe occurred: As I received my message from Kuan Yin and my "Anger ball" energy left my body, it landed on the lighter, which then continued to burn despite being disengaged from its fuel source. The lighter had absorbed the release of the pent-up energy my rage attracted. And the burning of the left half of the Hecate card was no accident.

I felt the magic of the universe all around me that day. I physically experienced the dangerous power of attracting negative energy and the amazing force of the ego to corrupt and destroy when feeling fear and judgment. The rage, the fight-or-flight instinct, and the blindness prevented me from seeing or receiving the gifts of the universe.

When I'd closed my eyes, I'd opened my heart, allowing it to connect with the Divine. I made the conscious choice then to step into compassion and love—to leave the warrior goddess I'd been behind, to thank her for her strength and service, and to step into the compassionate goddess I was becoming.

Ultimately, my brand coach and I easily designed the new approach for the three videos. We were in flow. The filming ran smoothly, and we remained wrapped in the arms of Kuan Yin throughout the remainder of the day.

Whether you believe in the energy of the universe or not, there is no denying that anger and fiery rage are contagious and spread like wildfire. As a counterpoint, love and compassion are also contagious and can spread from one person's moment of kindness to the person who receives it, and so on and so on. It can transform the world.

How can you choose love and compassion over judgment and anger? How can you choose to see a person's good intention instead of spinning or raging about words they chose that might sting you?

Awareness is pausing when the emotions surface. Taking a breath. Perhaps closing your eyes and asking your heart or the universe for guidance, then consciously choosing a path forward that honors who you want to be.

Awareness and Anger

Living by heart isn't about perfection, it's about practice. You won't always get it right. You won't always show up the way you want to. Situations may still trigger you and bring intense emotions to the surface.

What changes with a daily awareness practice is the speed with which you catch yourself. You'll notice the emotions bubbling earlier than before and, if you're lucky, stop the warrior before she strikes.

You can learn a lot about your warrior by examining her once she's sheathed her sword. When the warrior rage dies down and the fire goes out, there's time to reflect on the events that transpired. It's hard to look at a situation with openness and curiosity when the fire's still hot. So, give it some time to cool and come back when you know all the embers have died and there's no chance the flames will reignite.

You can ask yourself some questions:

"What happened?"
"What was said that set off my emotions?"
"What was I angry about?"
"What could I have done differently?"

Like in healing and empathy, be prepared for what you might uncover when you explore awareness deeply. You may unearth more emotions. You might discover things that you don't really like to admit about yourself. It will probably get uncomfortable.

But that's where growth lives: on the other side of the discomfort; on the other side of fear. There is no growth without it, and you can't go around it. There are no shortcuts. If you want to understand yourself more wholly, you've got to go through the emotions and learnings to get to the other side.

Choosing to reflect from your heart instead of your head can help. If you are feeling judgment toward yourself, it's likely that your judger self is leading your awareness practice. Before you begin, take a moment to breathe and connect with your heart. Your heart will help you stay open and curious instead of critical and judgy.

Years after my day at the video shoot, I did a deep dive to understand the rage I'd felt with the fire and Kuan Yin. Why had I been so angry?

This question invites a broader exploration into my soul and the anger it has carried, perhaps through many lifetimes. It comes from deep within me. It is powerful. It can be a little scary. It sometimes feels like an out-of-body experience because the rage can take over, leaving me thinking, *What is happening right now?*

This is the warrior within me.
When she feels hurt, she rages.
When she feels judged, she rages.

When she feels threatened or at risk in any way, where other parts of me might flee or freeze, she puts on her armor and charges into battle.

Why is my warrior so strong? So fierce?
Why is she ready to rise and challenge at any moment?
How did she develop? How does she serve me?

When I was growing up, I saw my sister as the "anger ball" and myself as the calm antagonizer. More generally, while my warrior self loved to argue and debate, I never really thought of myself as an "anger ball." I earned that title when I became a parent. There is so much to curiously explore here.

I've always been strong and determined. I've powerfully used my voice to command attention, to argue, defend, and influence others to my way of thinking. Perhaps, however, I've forced others to submit to my way of thinking. It sounds awful to say that out loud.

Who is the scared little girl behind the raging warrior?
That is what shows up when I sit with her.
Who is that scared little girl? What is she so afraid of?

If I step into the rage I was feeling that day now, I can see that I was angry because I felt stupid. I was angry because I felt like I'd wasted my time. I was angry because what my coach was saying made no sense to me.

I was angry because I impulsively thought I could do it better on my own. I was angry at myself for trusting someone else who let me down. I'd placed her on a pedestal with expectations for who I wanted her to be, on my terms. My comparison self said, *See, when you trust other people, this is what happens.*

I was angry because I felt attacked and judged. I felt like she was saying that I obviously didn't get it, that I was dumb. I felt like my intelligence was in question, and that felt personal. I was taking it very personally. *Hello, Judger self.*

In returning to that moment, those feelings stream back into my energetic field. I feel the desire I felt to quit and walk out the door. I just wanted to throw my hands up, say "F*ck this!" *Hello, Warrior self.*

The truth is that she didn't say any of the things I was angry about. Those thoughts were all created within me. I turned "this won't work" into "you're stupid."

I also carried an expectation of perfection for myself. I anticipated receiving praise from her for the amazing quality of my work. Instead, it felt like I received the opposite. Despite her actual words, what I heard was "it's totally wrong and won't work at all." Can you see how my whole Itty Bitty Sh*tty Committee was activated?

So, I went from feeling proud of the work I'd put together to feeling shattered in an instant. What's fascinated me about the event is how I raged inside yet shut down externally. I just remember looking at her, fire burning in my eyes. I could feel the fire burning! And I said nothing. I just looked at her.

What prevented me from expressing that rage? Releasing it versus containing it until it exploded like a grenade filled with shrapnel, injuring everything within a hundred-foot radius? Typically, my rage comes out of me through a string of scathing words that wound those in its path. Especially if I am hurt. *Hello, Warrior self.*

Gosh, you sound like a delightful human being. Thanks, Judger self.

What would happen if there was no judgment? Just acceptance of what is, without assigning meaning to it, without assigning good or bad, darkness or light? What would happen if I simply considered all of it as information?

This is where my heart lives. This is the connection to my higher self and the Divine. My heart guides me to release from the meaning making and just sit in the moment. She invites me to ask, *What am I meant to learn from this? What is the emotion of anger telling me?*

When I shift to my heart, I can see things differently. I can see myself and all my nuances with love and compassion. My heart invites me to give myself permission to be human, without apology. What I am experiencing is real and valid and worthy.

Yes. I am worthy.

I can transform the information that I receive from my anger.

My anger told me I put a lot of work into this.

My anger told me that it hurt to feel that my work wasn't what was needed for that project.

My heart told me that while it wasn't what was needed in the moment, that didn't make the work less worthy.

My heart told me that the moment didn't make me less worthy.

My heart told me that it was great work and could serve elsewhere.

And more work is needed.

All these things were true.

Sitting in that seat, looking at the world through that lens, brings love and kindness to everything. This is the gift of living by my heart.

My heart holds no judgment, only love. She makes no meaning, she just accepts what is. She holds no expectations, only possibilities.

The possibility of writing a new story and finding a harmonious way forward—this is where the inner work lives and where you can see that living by heart isn't linear. Exploring awareness may uncover more opportunities for your healing. Exploring awareness may bring you into greater empathy. Awareness may leap you forward into resilience or trust.

You won't know until you start the work.

Breathing into My Heart

In Empathy, I encouraged you to explore different modalities to connect with your heart. A Reiki session might uncover a block you're carrying in your throat chakra that suddenly frees your voice. An EFT session may have you laughing maniacally as you dig into your own worthiness. Another modality I recommend is breathwork to connect with your body, your heart, and your soul.

There are many healing practitioners who include breathwork in their practice. As a coach, I talk about some basic breathing techniques with my clients like box breathing, which I explain in this book. For deeper breathwork, I recommend working with a certified breathwork instructor.

Curious to know more? My first deep breathwork experience led to an incredible opening in my own awareness.

"Have you ever done breathwork?" the breathwork practitioner asked me. I'd been at several meditation events where the host said we'd be doing some breathwork during the session, so I confirmed that I had. It would have been better if I'd asked for clarification, however. Not all "breathwork" is the same. Not all "breathwork" practitioners run a breathwork session in the same way. As it turned out, I was not ready for this activity.

During COVID, the only option for gathering for a breathwork session was through a virtual call. There were four participants from four separate locations, all calling in on a Zoom meeting. Our host, a fellow coach and trusted colleague, invited us to turn our cameras off and find a comfortable place to lie down.

It was the middle of summer, and I was at the cottage, so I retreated to my bedroom for some privacy. I closed the door and set my computer beside me on the bed, then plugged in my headphones so my family wouldn't hear the session.

The practitioner advised us that the breathwork session would be thirty minutes and that we should close our eyes. If at any time the breathing was too intense, she explained, we could slow down to our own pace. She told us that we may experience some emotions during the session and that it was all quite normal.

All I really wanted from this breathwork session was to feel some peace and relaxation. The summer had been very challenging by that point. I'd spent all of June and most of July trying to clear my mom's home of furniture and belongings she'd gathered over her lifetime. I was stressed.

Mom was restricted to her retirement residence, so I'd tried to balance including her virtually for significant decisions about her house. It was important to me that she felt some control over the process, with the immensity of the project and a tight timeline that required the ruthless disposal of items my mom didn't really care about. I'd driven back and forth from the city to the cottage, a drive that takes nearly three hours one direction, sometimes multiple times a week. I was emotionally and physically exhausted and ready for some healing.

The music started and the session began. Initially, my mind was busy with random thoughts, and I wondered whether this "breathwork thing" was really for me.

You need this, said my heart. I decided to stick with it and be open to the process.

As our breathing exercises intensified, I could feel some emotions surfacing. *Curious. How is this happening? Maybe it's just my exhaustion being released.*

"Two counts in. Two counts out," the practitioner instructed, then demonstrated. I felt myself take deeper breaths than I ever recalled taking before. Before long, the tears started rolling down my cheeks, big, fat tears that dripped into my ears.

Yep, I'm tired.

Suddenly I felt a "whoosh" of energy run down my body from the tip of my head to my toes. It was like an ocean wave flowing through me.

"Whoosh!" It happened again. More tears.

The waves seemed to wash out the weight I'd been carrying, releasing the pent-up emotions I'd been holding in for weeks.

"One count in, one count out," I heard our host say. I worried I might hyperventilate. I'd never breathed like this in my life.

I sobbed. It caught me by surprise. I was really crying hard now. It was difficult to keep breathing like this while crying. For a moment, I wondered whether any other participant on the call was experiencing this or if it was just me. *Hello, Comparison self!*

No one wants to see you like this, chimed in my judger self, commanding that I stop crying.

My heart then hugged my judger self and comparison self, and she thanked them.

Let it go, love. You're safe. Let it all go. So, I did.

"Make any sounds you want to make. If you want to sigh, moan, or yell, let it out," the practitioner said with encouragement. I hadn't considered making any sounds. My family was just in the next room. Would they be disturbed by it?

I found myself releasing long, loud sighs. The sighs reminded me of the panting breathing during delivery. My sighs were almost an octave in range, starting high, cresting like a wave, then going low. "Ahhhhhhhh. Ahhhhhhhh."

Our host invited us to yell: "Let your voice loose. Yell at the top of your lungs. Scream if you want to."

Despite my awareness of my surroundings, I felt supported and loved. So, I opened my mouth and screamed at the top of my lungs. My yell was so loud it scared me. Yet, none of my family members entered the room. I guess they were used to my meditation, chanting, and Tao song by then, so they weren't surprised to hear me screaming.

Oh, the sweet release that followed letting my voice loose. I cried uncontrollably then.

What was I so upset about? I had no idea what specifically was upsetting me, I just knew that the deep weight I'd been carrying was lifting. I could feel it leaving my body.

I knew that it was hard to honor my mom, ensure she felt involved, and still handle the pressure of doing all the work by myself. I felt judged when Mom questioned the decisions I'd made without her. I felt emotional when I had to make some difficult decisions Mom didn't want to make. I realized I was also feeling sad. Even though Mom was still alive, clearing her home without her there felt like I was saying goodbye to her. *Oh, I didn't know I felt that way.* No wonder I felt like I was carrying such a heavy weight!

The breathwork activity revealed many new insights and cleared my body so I could continue the work supporting my mom.

I tried to catch my breath. Sob, breath, breath, sob. My pillow was drenched beneath my head and my ears were filled with salty tears as our host slowly brought us back to box breathing to ground us. My tears stopped. My breathing began normalizing, and I felt lighter.

"Take your time. Roll on to your side if you'd like before opening your eyes."

I put my arms above my head and stretched. How did my body feel so relaxed and rejuvenated? I couldn't believe how refreshed I felt.

"How was it?" she asked.

"Amazing," I replied. "I realized during this session that I've never really done breathwork before. I really needed this. Thank you."

There is so much wisdom in your body, in your heart, and in your soul that you can connect with by exploring different modalities like breathwork, Reiki, EFT, dance, yoga, and meditation. I encourage you to explore which activities help you connect with your body in addition to participating in your own daily awareness practices. Awareness starts with curiosity, and adding a small dose of playfulness can enhance your learning about yourself.

Get curious and have fun unlocking new awareness through connecting with your body.

Awareness as a Practice

Awareness is a practice that truly never ends. There are more tools and techniques you can use to learn about yourself than you could try out in one lifetime. Don't get overwhelmed. Test out one or two activities you're curious about first. Give them time to become habits before you add another activity. And if something you try really doesn't work for you, let it go. There are plenty of options available.

To keep it simple, I've highlighted my top three self-awareness practices. You can do these by yourself anywhere at any time.

INNER CRITIC WORK:

The inner critic is one of the first topics we talk about when I start working with a new coaching client. We start here because while we all have at least one inner critic voice that gets in our way, many people aren't aware that this voice is separate from other parts of ourselves.

Separating that voice, identifying it, and even naming it (if you want to) can disempower your inner critic and let you step more confidently into control over your thoughts and life.

If you've already done some work with your inner critic, or if you've already identified your whole IBSC like I have, you may choose to move to the next activity or alternatively, spend a short period of time now reviewing what you know about it. See if anything has changed. Each time I check in on my IBSC, I discover new phrases my committee has created to try to take me off course. They are so sneaky!

If this is new work for you, I encourage you to invest some time in getting to know your inner critic. Ask yourself: "Who is my inner critic? What do they look like?" You can then draw your inner critic on a piece of paper or, if you're feeling creative, build your inner critic with materials like construction paper, markers, scissors, glue or tape, googly eyes, yarn, popsicle sticks, feathers, or glitter.

After you've created your inner critic, you can name it, if you haven't already. Have fun with this! Choose a name that takes some of its power away.

Now, consider a phrase (or two) that you hear your inner critic say to you. It can be helpful to write the phrase down on paper. Writing it down can get it out of your head and separate from you so you can see it and observe it externally.

For me, doing this activity multiple times over the years helped me discover that I had a whole committee of critics, the IBSC, who showed up at different times to get in my way. This work also helped me understand that while my ego and my warrior have each helped me succeed at times in my life, they are part of my IBSC and are often in my way.

I discovered the most recent member of my IBSC through this work—"The Diva." When I imagined what she looked like, I created her with a big face mounted on a popsicle stick with a huge mouth that's wide open because she's always criticizing me. She's got curly hair and blue eyes with big lashes. The Diva shows up when I'm feeling uncomfortable in social situations or when I'm in the spotlight and not trusting myself.

While your inner critic, or IBSC if you have more than one, can seem cruel and get in your way often, the more you get to know it, the better you can appreciate their desire to protect you. Give love to them, thank them graciously, then invite them to step back so you can bring your authentic self to your work and your life.

HEART WORK:

Once you've gotten to know your inner critic or critics, dedicate some time getting to know the voice of your heart. Your heart can be a powerful resource to support your shift from inner critic into your whole, authentic self, the self that believes in you, has your back, and can be your greatest cheerleader.

Initially, you may find that pausing to take a few deep breaths or playing a song that inspires you may actually help you connect with the voice of your heart. I like to put one hand over my heart to help me focus and tune into it.

Test out different activities to find out what works best for you. If you feel yourself spinning in a state of overwhelm, taking a moment to pause before you ask your heart for answers can be helpful.

Once calm and present, check in with your heart.

"What does my heart say about this?"
"What does my heart want?"
"What does my heart know?"

If you're feeling emotions like sadness, anger, or worry, you can check in with your heart for information without judgment.

"What is this emotion telling me?"
"What do I need right now?"
"What does my heart see or hear from this emotion I'm feeling?"

It takes time to be able to work with your inner critic and your heart in the moment. Initially, it may feel clunky and unnatural. I experienced a lot of judgment about myself when I started this work, because even though I knew and understood my IBSC, they still got the better of me a lot and I hated that. I believed that I should be better at managing those voices once I discovered them. I didn't realize it was a practice that develops over time.

Be kind to yourself as you start this work. There is no such thing as perfection. Just work toward increasing your own awareness and your ability to catch your inner critic more quickly in the moment so you can shift into your heart.

AWARENESS REFLECTION PRACTICE:

Whether through journaling, meditation, or other reflection activity you've chosen from testing what works best for you in the Healing and Empathy practices we've talked about, a key aspect to growth in your awareness of yourself comes from having a regular reflective practice.

In the early days of my own awareness work, I only journaled about what I was aware of in the evenings. It was a "looking back" practice where I'd check in with questions such as:

"What did I learn about myself today?"
"Where did my inner critic show up today?"
"How did my heart support me today?"

As I learned more about my judger self, my ego, and my comparison self, I started setting more intentions at the start of my day in my morning journaling practice.

I'd look at the upcoming activities for the day and ask myself:

"What challenges do I anticipate today where my ego might get in the way?"

"Who am I interacting with that I tend to compare myself to? How will I lead with compassion and love for them and for myself?"

"What do I already feel judgment about as I look at my day? How do I want to show up differently today?"

There are no right questions to ask, just questions that work well for you to gain more awareness and insights about yourself.

Test out the questions I've provided to get started or create your own questions if you wish.

Reflection isn't about getting it "right" or about perfection. Notice which part of you keeps you striving for perfection. Is it your ego or judger self? Reflection from your heart is about figuring out what works best for you in this moment. My reflective practice continues to evolve as I learn and grow. Questions I used to ask myself regularly and got comfortable with I've replaced with more challenging questions I find harder to answer.

Growth in yourself doesn't happen in the comfort zone. If you get too comfortable, you've likely stopped growing.

RESILIENCE

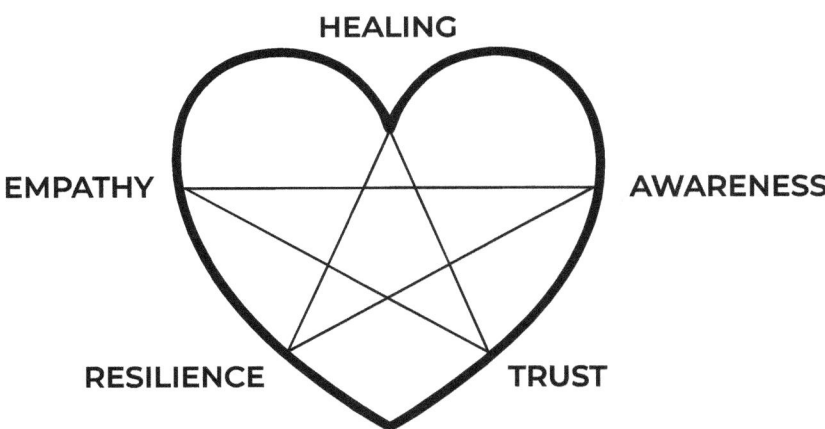

HEALING

EMPATHY

AWARENESS

RESILIENCE

TRUST

What Is Resilience?

Take a moment to pause and think about what resilience means to you. What's important about it? Is resilience something you know you have? Or perhaps it's something you desire to have more of? What would having more resilience give you?

In 2024 it seemed like everyone was talking about building resilience. It's the leadership skill du jour. Coaching clients came to me saying, "I need to build resilience," and in curiosity, I'd ask them what that meant. Most people weren't sure, they just knew they needed it, and they didn't think they had it. Before we started working on building their resilience, I invited them to ask themselves questions to better understand what they were wanting and what having resilience would give them that they didn't believe they currently had.

To me, resilience is the ability to bounce back after falling. It is the willingness to get up, to keep going, even when it feels like the odds are stacked against you. Resilience includes the belief that "this too shall pass," and that the pain in this moment is temporary. It's the belief that fuels the action to get up and keep moving.

When I started working on resilience, it was different from the inward focus of healing and awareness, and the outward focus of empathy. In resilience, I applied the tools I'd already learned on the journey to test my thinking, explore barriers, and understand how to fuel my resilience. I noticed that it felt different writing about resilience too. You may find this section of the book feels different than the previous practices of Living by HEART. I invite you to explore it with openness and curiosity and see what you discover about your own resilience.

What if I told you that you were born resilient? Do you feel agreement for or resistance to that idea? I believe you were, indeed, born resilient. I believe we all were. If you need some evidence, consider the resilience of a baby.

A newborn baby, having no words to tell the world what she needs, keeps trying with different cries until someone figures it out. A six-month-old teething baby chews on his fingers and rubs his blanket to soothe himself until the discomfort passes. A one-year-old keeps taking steps and falling until she masters walking without assistance. How did all these infants know to not give up? They were born resilient.

Yet somehow along the way we disconnected from our resilience, or we forgot we had resilience when we got here. I can't explain what happened, but I know your resilience still lives within you. She's just dormant.

If you agree that you were born resilient, you know deep within your soul how to bounce back and keep going. Let's spend some time tapping into your own innate resilience and looking at how to fuel your resilience so it carries you through the challenging times ahead.

Past and Present

Resilience isn't a conscious act. You don't look at a list of skills and say, "I'm going to select resilience now." It is unconscious, the same way a baby doesn't consciously choose to keep crying until her needs are met. She just does it, because it's innate. As an adult, your resilience kicks in and takes over when you're in crisis.

You're more likely to look back at an event and realize how resilient you were during that challenge than you are to say, "I hope I have the resilience needed to get through the challenge ahead."

You can poke your head up when you're in the middle of a sh*tstorm and notice that you're using a lot of resilience to get through it, but you're more likely to say, "I have no idea how I'm getting through it; I just keep going."

Take a moment to reflect on some of the challenging times you've experienced in your life. As you look back, do you see how resilience showed up to support you? Maybe you feel you could have used a bit more, or maybe you're surprised to discover you had just what you needed.

Today, I know I have innate resilience within me. But sometimes, in the hard times, I still doubt her strength. As I've shared, I've grown more as a parent in the last two years than I did in the previous eighteen. Due to recent challenges in our family, we're journeying together in a marathon. To say I've needed resilience is an understatement.

I never learned to run a marathon. The longest distance I ran before I tore my ACL in 2013 and ended my brief running career was ten kilometers, a substantial distance for someone who grew up believing she couldn't run at all. Perhaps if I had prepared to run a marathon, I would be more prepared for the marathon that is currently my life.

"Oh Heather, don't be so dramatic!" I hear my mom's voice in my head.

Seriously, though. I don't think it's dramatic to say we are currently in the marathon of our lives and perhaps only at mile two, which seems dreadfully, painfully sad. If we're only at mile two of a twenty-six-mile marathon, how long will the other twenty-four miles take? Harder still is the awareness that we may be in an ultra-marathon, not a traditional one, and we have no way of knowing.

You're likely asking, "What the heck is she talking about?"

His story isn't mine to tell. But my story is inextricably linked to his. My story is heavily influenced by his story. He is part of my story. I have learned so much about living by heart through this leg of the journey, and while I seriously debated about leaving it out, to do so would be a disservice to you and to me.

So, here's what I can say. All my sons experienced challenges having to live through COVID. Most parents I speak to say the same. We likely won't know the extent of the impact COVID had on this generation of young people for years, but we can see the evidence of the fallout all around us. One of my sons had an extremely hard time and has since battled with mental health and substance use challenges.

It's been a roller-coaster ride. I've had to learn to become the parent he needs, not the parent I thought I should be. I've had to learn to let go of what I cannot control and focus on what's mine to own. I've had to learn to take care of myself so that I can love and support him, and all my family members, on this journey. It's been exhausting.

"No one would blame you if you quit."

No one said this to me out loud. But I heard it underneath their words when people told me that my exhaustion made sense to them. They said they didn't know how I kept going. They couldn't imagine how hard it was.

I know they said these words with care, compassion, and with the best intentions. But the more people said it, the more furious and determined I became. I suppose on some level, I should thank them. Perhaps my anger at their words got me through the hardest moments. Their words brought out the warrior in me.

Proving them wrong.
Proving I was strong.
Proving I was resilient.
Proving I could "do hard things."

"We can do hard things." *Oh, god!* My least favorite Glennon Doyle expression. And I love her. I really do. But something about that quote just rubs me the wrong way. I know it's meant to inspire people, but it doesn't inspire me. It just makes me more furious. I don't want to do more hard things, thank you very much.

While I don't like the expression "we can do hard things," I must admit that I've done a lot of hard things since my living by heart journey began back in 2012.

Raising three sons, nurturing a marriage, and juggling the challenges of being in the sandwich generation, all while both Jason and I worked full-time and built our careers, was hard.

Giving everything I had to my work, at the expense of myself, was hard.

Changing roles at work, only to have the new role eliminated and thus leaving an organization I grew up with and loved, was hard.

Setting up and running my own business, knowing the only one I was accountable to was myself, was hard.

Living through COVID when all my scheduled business disappeared, and my office disappeared, and my family was on top of me at every moment and I felt like I was failing in absolutely every aspect of my life all at once, was hard.

Taking care of Mom first while she lived on her own, then moving her into a retirement residence, and then clearing, renovating, and selling her house during COVID was hard.

Watching my mother-in-law courageously live her life on her terms for four years while she navigated ovarian cancer. Being so inspired by her and so angry at the universe for putting this incredible human through this unimaginable thing that would ultimately take her way too soon was hard.

Learning my mom had stage four of the very same cancer just three weeks after my mother-in-law passed was impossibly hard.

Supporting my mom through her illness and putting my business on hold to spend as much time with her as I could was hard.

Grieving her for almost a year after her passing was shocking and hard.

Feeling ready to rise again after the grief started to subside, only to be beaten down, shocked to my core, and terrified out of my mind, then starting the marathon of my life has been unbearably hard.

When you love someone close to you and you can't help them.

When you watch someone battle with addiction and their own demons, and you know you can only offer them love and wait until they are ready to make different choices. It is incredibly hard.

Then losing my dad to dementia, watching him suffer, and learning that he passed away during one of the most challenging weeks in our family marathon seemed almost comical after the journey of hard things so far.

Yet I'm still here.
I'm still standing.
I'm still living and loving and growing.

So, I don't care if no one would blame me if I quit.

I won't quit.

I don't quit.

I will seek out every opportunity for growth in every challenge I face and rise again.

I will look at each misstep, each roadblock, each boulder I keep pushing up hill, as a chance to learn something.

Yes, Warrior!

This is what resilience looks like to me.

What does it look like for you? As you look at the challenging moments in your own life, do you see your own resilience? Do you see the warrior within you picking you up, brushing you off, maybe giving you a quick hug, and sending you on your way?

Living by heart doesn't eliminate the challenges you'll face in your life, it connects you to the innate resilience within your soul so you can navigate the hard stuff with love, compassion, determination, grit, and some grace.

How do you tap into that part of yourself? Reflection can be a great way to tap into your resilience. It's through reflection that you can spot when she's shown up for you in the past and how you can access her in the future.

When I reflect on my own life, I see what I've been through in my first fifty years. I'll be damned if I let life take me down now! No, sir. Not happening.

See. She's right there, beside me. Just like she's right beside you.

Reflection helps me tap into her strength and understand her better. My resilience is a part of me that I always had. When I picture her, I see my eight-year-old self.

She's the eight-year-old me who was never told that quitting was an option.

She's the eight-year-old me who believed in miracles and magic.

She's the eight-year-old me who knew she could take on the world and thrive.

Man, I love that eight-year-old me.

Thank you for showing up and having my back.

What do you see when you picture your own resilience? What's the image that comes to your mind? Your resilience could be an image of yourself, another figure, or even an object that represents how you see the resilience. Sit with that image for a moment. If you're seeing it for the first time, give yourself a few minutes to take it in. Say hello. Give it some love and gratitude. Your resilience has been within you your whole life.

I don't believe resilience is something you develop or something you grow. You came out of the womb a fighter, a survivor, with all the resilience you needed to make it in life. But at some point, during your journey, someone told you that you didn't have it. Someone told you resilience was something you needed to get or build. Something happened that made you question whether you could handle what life gives you.

You don't need crisis to prove you're resilient.
You don't need a loved one to be struggling with addiction.
You don't need to be grieving a death.
You were born resilient.
I was born resilient.
We just forgot that it was already within us.
It's my responsibility to connect with that part of myself.
It's your responsibility to connect with yours.
Nourish her. Take care of her.
Give her rest.
Give her love.

Give her space and grace and a place to hang her coat so she can stay for a while.

Resilience, Pregnancy, and Parenthood

At every life stage and milestone event, society seems to have standard questions to ask you. When you finish school, you're asked what you want to do for a living. When you start dating, you're asked if you want to get married. And if you get married, the next standard question is whether (or when!) you'll have children.

These questions create expectations of what your life "should" look like, what the measures of success "should" be, and what you "should" want. What they don't prepare you for in any way is what you'll need to navigate the challenges that come from work, marriage, children, and the countless choices you make along the way.

By twenty-five, I knew that I wanted to have and raise kids with Jason. Coming from a two-kid family, I also knew I didn't want just two kids. And I didn't want three kids, as I believed there would always be an "odd man out." My dream number was four kids.

Looking back at my dream of raising four kids makes me chuckle now. *What was I thinking?!*

The number of times I have said "I didn't sign up for this" since my kids were born is too many to count. The thing is, I did sign up to be a parent. In fact, I raised my hand and jumped around so the universe would notice me.

I believe in the power of the universe and to "ask for what you want." It's great advice for all aspects of life. In this case, I wanted four children, and I wanted them to be relatively close in age, but not too close. The universe listened and answered. It has a sense of humor.

After the birth of our first son, we waited a few years before deciding to try for our second child. During that time, a few different couples we knew who had been trying to conceive their second told us it was taking longer than they'd expected.

I got nervous; Jason got excited. He looked forward to having "lots of practice" for baby number two. So, we both agreed to start "trying." (I write "trying" in quotations because I am 98 percent confident that we got pregnant for the second time on our very first try.)

We started a two-week vacation a few weeks later, and on the drive to the cottage, I noticed I was feeling nauseated. I joked that I might be pregnant already. Neither of us took my joke seriously. But after two days at the lake, I was barely able to eat or partake in the dock-side cocktails that I normally enjoyed. We headed into town to pick up a pregnancy test. Sure enough, I was pregnant. Jason was quite disappointed that he hadn't gotten more "practice."

In the early weeks of my second pregnancy, a few strange things happened:

At a local BBQ event, I met a woman who had just learned she was having twins.

"How exciting!" I exclaimed. She didn't look convinced. Thinking I was being helpful, I added, "The universe doesn't give you anything you can't handle."

The following week, a friend called me in a panic. She had a plant that flowered whenever someone she knew got pregnant, and it had flowered again.

"Oh my god," she said. "My plant has its first ever double-flower! And I just found out I'm pregnant. What if I'm having twins?" I could hear the terror in her voice.

Still certain it was helpful, I offered my advice for a second time. "The universe doesn't give us anything we can't handle. If it happens, you've got this!"

A few days later, I called my dad to finalize plans for our upcoming trip to visit him in San Diego. "I can be the designated driver," I told him. "I won't be drinking on this trip."

"Does this mean you're pregnant?" Dad asked.
"It does," I said.
"Congratulations. Boy or girl?" he asked.
"I don't know yet."
"Single or multiple?" he asked.
"What a strange question, Dad!" *What made him ask me that?*

Six weeks into my pregnancy, I was scheduled for my first appointment with our obstetrician. I told Jason he didn't need to come to the appointment. We knew what to expect. We'd done this before.

The doctor had an ultrasound machine in his office and as he checked for the baby's heartbeat, he said, "Here's the heartbeat of your baby. And here's the heartbeat of your other baby."

I'm sorry, what?!

I asked him to please repeat what he'd said because I must have misheard him. He confirmed we were having twins. Then he launched into details of everything I needed to know for a multiple pregnancy. I didn't hear a word he said. All I kept hearing was "Here's the heartbeat of your baby. And here's the heartbeat of your other baby."

Then I heard my own "helpful" words I'd offered to two other pregnant women echoing in my ears. "The universe doesn't give you anything you can't handle." Had I unconsciously known I was pregnant with twins and was thus giving myself advice? Or did the universe just have a twisted sense of humor? Either way, I was going to need resilience to navigate parenthood from here.

I didn't realize I'd need resilience right away for the barrage of unwanted questions that inevitably came with being pregnant with twins. Throughout my pregnancy, I was frequently asked well-meaning but intrusive questions such as "Are you pregnant with twins naturally?"

I think people are fearful of pregnancies with multiples. To reduce their fear, they hoped to hear that my pregnancy was assisted in some way. Multiples are "expected" with IVF, for example. But my response didn't calm their fears as I patiently told them my multiple pregnancy occurred the "natural" way.

"Do twins run in your family?" This was the follow-up question as people sought reassurance that this couldn't happen to them. Interestingly, twins did run in Jason's family. But as our twins were fraternal, meaning two separate eggs were fertilized at the same time, his genetics couldn't make my body release two eggs at one time. That was all me.

My twin pregnancy proceeded relatively smoothly, but as we neared the delivery date, more people asked more questions, and I grew more tired answering them. Each day I called on my heart to give me strength so I could show up with love, compassion, and patience for the genuinely well-intentioned people who pushed, prodded, and poked at me with their curiosity.

After the twins were born, Jason and I both felt that the risk of another multiple pregnancy was just too high. I abandoned my dream of four kids to ensure we didn't end up raising five, six, or seven kids. A good call, because parenting three young boys was challenge enough.

The first six months were a complete blur. I spent a lot of time crying and often fell asleep with a baby in each arm and tear-stained cheeks. It was so hard!

One day, my father-in-law remarked how he was sure I was documenting the parenting journey because I always journaled so diligently. Guilt washed over me. I hadn't journaled once since before the twins were born! I was determined to start journaling again. I decided to start by capturing one day in the life with twins and a toddler. It took me three days to write that one entry.

While frustrated at how long it took me to write it, what this entry showed me was just how resilient I'd been during the day-to-day stresses of trying to keep everyone clean, fed, and loved. I could see the strength I didn't know I had and certainly didn't feel.

The next five years of parenting three highly energetic, inquisitive, and independently minded boys tested me physically, mentally, and emotionally. I had many "mom fails," many times when I thought, *I didn't sign up for this*. But the resilience I was born with kept picking me up, dusting me off, and giving me a quick hug. "You've got this. Get back in the ring," it would say.

The old programming of "not good enough" can prevent you from seeing your own resilience. It keeps your strength hidden beneath a cloak of all the flaws. Notice if you learned to focus on what's wrong, instead of what's strong.

Reconnecting with your innate resilience brings your strengths into the light. If you haven't stopped to notice your own resilience, take a pause now and look at the times when you were strong that perhaps you didn't see at the time. Celebrate them.

Comparison Kills Resilience

Who do you compare yourself to? Perhaps you compare yourself to the friend or colleague who always looks like they have all their stuff together. Perhaps you compare yourself to earlier versions of yourself, versions you believe were better than you think you are now.

Every client I've worked with suffers from some form of "comparison-itis." I've had my share of suffering from it too. Why do we compare ourselves so much?

I remember the first time I heard the sentiment "Comparison is the thief of joy," often attributed to Theodore Roosevelt. It struck a chord deep within me. I heard my heart shout *YES!* and for the first time, I could see how my habit of comparing myself to others and to earlier versions of myself caused me harm and pain.

I repeat this sentiment with all my clients when they share a comparison they're making. Sometimes they don't even realize they are comparing themselves to something, or that they can choose not to. Many clients keep a copy of the sentiment with them to remind them about losing joy when their own comparison thief creeps back in.

I've carried it with me for almost ten years now. I carry it as a reminder that when I compare myself to others, I steal my own joy. The warrior in me used to think that comparing myself fueled my fire to do more, do better, or to be the best. Not bad things to aspire to, right?

On one hand, my striving paid off many times over. When I left university without a degree, I compared myself to successful leaders who had degrees and emulated what I perceived made those leaders great. That hard work and dedication led to promotions and opportunities to do work I never imagined myself doing.

But living in a constant state of comparison prevented me from being present in my life. I didn't celebrate my own successes because I always needed to do better. It was never enough. My "comparison-itis" stripped me of the joy I should have experienced along the way.

I did a lot of work on myself in those early years to free myself from the chains of comparison-itis and instead measure myself against my own yardstick. I journaled and asked myself questions like "Who was I before compared to who I am now?" I felt energy from that reflection. I celebrated how far I'd come and where I was heading. This shift in my focus allowed me to be in the moment and feel more joy in my life.

And it worked, for a while.

Then, when changes at work resulted in me leaving my company after eighteen years, the old framework I'd built to manage my comparison-itis wasn't as helpful. For eighteen years I'd defined myself, my success and my worthiness, primarily through my work.

Sounds strange, doesn't it? After all the inner work I'd done, building up my self-love, embracing empathy and compassion toward others, understanding my ego and learning to shift into curiosity, why did this change feel like such a monumental setback?

Maybe you've had moments in your own journey that feel like major setbacks. You get to a specific point, then an event sends you spinning and you feel like you've spiraled back to somewhere you didn't think you'd return to.

What's hard to see in that moment is that you are never the same person you previously were. Even if you return to a spot on the map that looks familiar, every step you took between when you first left that spot until now has changed you. Each new experience, insight, and all the growth along the way changed you. You aren't the same, so therefore you can't ever really return to the same spot.

I couldn't see that at first when I left the company I'd grown up with, and I liken leaving an organization I loved to that of the pain over a marital breakup. Yes, I know, I'm making a comparison. The irony isn't lost on me. But it truly is the best way to describe what I felt.

My identity was wrapped up in the company I'd represented for almost twenty years. The company was a part of me, and I felt I was a part of it, so when that relationship ended, I experienced the five stages of grief that usually occur with the death of a loved one or the end of a marriage.

To get me through that difficult time, I leaned into my heart and embraced the vision I had of a phoenix rising from the ashes. I'd rise fully transformed into a new version of myself and launch my own coaching and training business. I could see it, taste it, sense it. I tapped into my warrior and my heart together. They rose as one compassionate warrior to guide me. I dreamed, created, and executed my vision for myself, and I felt strong, for a while.

When it came time to completely release my corporate identity, I kept finding threads that tied me to the woman I was when I worked there. She was amazing! She had strong friendships at work. She was highly regarded. She was an expert in her field. Who was this woman before me staring back in the mirror?

It took me eighteen months to stop referring to that company as "we." I remember the moment it happened.

On a warm and sunny June day, I sat on the patio of a delightful restaurant with a dear friend I'd worked with during my corporate years. We chatted like excited schoolgirls, catching up on all the news and things we were working on. There was hardly a breath between sentences. Sometimes we talked over each other, as if there wasn't enough time to say everything we wanted to share.

I made a comment about the company. Halfway into my next sentence, I heard myself say "they" and stopped abruptly. "Oh my god!" I exclaimed.

"What?" my friend asked, concerned.

"I finally referred to the company as THEY!"

She looked a little confused.

"It's taken me over eighteen months to stop calling them 'we.' I just called them THEY. I'm so excited!"

My friend could tell how important this moment was for me. She ordered a bottle of prosecco so we could celebrate.

After eighteen months of grieving, releasing, and transforming into the new version of "me" I wanted to be, I'd reached the pinnacle. I was there.

There was only one problem. Deep beneath the surface, I still believed that the old version of myself was better than any new version ever could be. As time passed, I propped that old version up higher and higher on a pedestal. The old "self-actualized, living by heart, gainfully employed in a high-profile role at a highly respected organization" version.

As resilient as I was navigating through the grief and transformation, I carried that version of myself in my pocket to pull out and remind me of who I used to be whenever I thought I was having the slightest inkling of success.

Oh, my Itty Bitty Sh*tty Committee is so damn sneaky! It wasn't until I started writing this book that I could see just how sneaky the IBSC truly was—how I kept unconsciously holding on to this older version of myself and how it was keeping me small.

As I built my business, I kept taking courses to improve my coaching skills. I took marketing and social media courses, courses to improve my training skills, and any other course I thought would make me better than that older version of myself that I idolized. Only I didn't realize what I was doing.

"When I complete this course, I can reach out to more prospective clients."

"When I have this designation, I can ask for more money."

"When I'm certified with this assessment tool, I'll be better able to market myself."

More insipid ways my IBSC told me I'd never be as good as I used to be. The truth is that all the great qualities I'd built in my corporate role, and all the inner, living by heart work I'd done on myself, it all came with me when I left.

But nostalgia and my putting an idolized version of my old self up on a pedestal got in the way of seeing all the incredible parts of my past I brought with me and loving the new version I'd transformed into.

Is there a version of you that's keeping you stuck? A version you might be holding on to? Or is there a version of you that you're striving to be? A version you've placed on a pedestal that keeps you feeling like you'll never be enough?

Comparison doesn't just steal your joy. Comparison also kills your resilience. It drains you of the energy your heart, body, and mind need to navigate the challenging terrain ahead. Together, let's knock down those pedestals, shatter the idols we've created, and choose to focus on the remarkable human you are right now.

Draining and Fueling Resilience

You can create, edit, and delete the stories you tell yourself, the stories you tell about yourself, in the same way you can write a story for a book.

In my work with my coaching clients, we often explore these stories. The mind is such a powerful tool that it can take an event, interpret it based on how it perceived that event, and create a story or narrative for that event. Sometimes that story plays on repeat in their mind, creating certainty that the event occurred exactly how they remember it.

The problem is that while our own perception is our reality, it isn't necessarily fact. If you put four people in a room and play a short film for the group, then discuss it together, it's remarkable how the same film is interpreted differently by the four people who sat in the very same room, in the very same moment, watching the very same thing. How does that happen?

Your mind is influenced by past experiences, beliefs, values, opinions of the people involved, and more. As a result, your mind assigns meaning to the events in your life based on all the unique traits that make up who you are.

When it comes to comparison, this makes everything much more complicated. What you perceive to be true is unlikely to be fact. When you compare yourself to someone else, your mind chooses a sliver of data based not only on what you observe but also all the meaning your mind makes of the data, then creates a perception.

The same is true about the memories we hold about ourselves. Our mind makes meaning of those memories and can edit, delete, or change our perception of the facts.

Brené Brown, in her book *Daring Greatly*, claims nostalgia is a dangerous form of comparison. She asks us to consider how our nostalgia can "edit" our memories to create an experience that never actually happened.

Wow! When I started writing this book, I believed I was journeying "back" to this person I used to be, someone I'd placed on a pedestal because I'd edited that version of myself to only remember the best parts. I believed I was a "better" person than I am now, and I wanted to get back to something—a time when I felt at my best.

But I've been living by heart this whole time. The past self I wanted to be evolved into the amazing human that I honor and respect now. Gosh, she's been through so much!

If you are trying to get back to an earlier version of yourself, I invite you to consider how nostalgia and your mind may have edited your memory. Did you strip out all the struggle and leave only the best parts? How is that memory serving you? If it isn't, let it go. Trust that the person you are now evolved from the versions of yourself in the past. You don't lose those parts, you grow from them into the next great version of yourself. What if who you are now is exactly who you're supposed to be?

As I contemplated this possibility for myself, I reflected on all the inner healing work that I've done. All the work on developing and embodying empathy, and not just knowing what it is but living it daily. All the inner work to become aware, and the resulting self-management work and relationship work that's followed. My resilience practice (and it is a practice!), and finally, learning to trust myself and others.

That work didn't end while navigating the last five challenging years.

It didn't stop when my mother-in-law died.

It didn't stop when my mom died.

It didn't stop when we faced mental health challenges and addiction as a family.

In fact, my living by heart only got stronger.

What I discovered by reflecting, however, was one part of my Living by HEART practice I didn't prioritize. The one part of Living by HEART that I found difficult to maintain over the past five years was ensuring I took good care of myself. I put that part on hold for a while, and my physical, mental, and emotional health suffered.

I've noticed that most of my coaching clients make the same choice when faced with stressful, challenging times. They put all their energy into taking care of everyone and everything else and put themselves last. At their own expense. And while it's okay for a week or two, putting care for yourself on hold for extended periods of time ends up impacting everyone else around you eventually.

Almost a year after my mom passed away and I'd worked through the deepest part of my grief, I finally went to see my family doctor. I had a few concerns about my own physical health that I'd put off during COVID and then while caring for Mom. At my appointment, I learned that I had high cholesterol and needed to change how I was taking care of myself. I learned that in addition to diet, stress is a major contributor to high cholesterol, and I was trying to juggle way too many things.

So, I looked at everything I had on my plate and determined what to cut back on. It was hard to admit that while I loved my extracurricular activities, they added to my stress, so I stepped back from all of them.

It was difficult for me to let people down. I'd made commitments and taken on roles that my departure would leave others having to fill. I felt awful when I called each person to tell them about the tough choice I'd made. Guilt was heavy, and my IBSC had a heyday over it.

But my heart said, *Love, you can't be resilient when you need to be if you're exhausted and burnt out*. She was right. After feeling guilty, sad, and out of integrity during those phone calls, I felt calmer, more at peace, and better able to breathe.

You may have commitments that don't serve or fuel you. Part of fueling your resilience is scaling back on the activities that drain your energy, wherever you can. Of course, there will be some energy-draining activities you can't eliminate, but I encourage you to take stock of all you have on your plate and see where you can clear some space.

While I was born resilient, nourishment and rest played vital roles in ensuring I was fueled up to navigate the daily stressors I faced. I paid closer attention to what I was eating, drinking, and how I was sleeping. I noticed that even a single glass of wine or cup of coffee after 3 p.m. impacted how I slept at night. Thus, when I was under stressful periods of time, I limited myself to a single coffee in the morning and wine only on weekends if life was calm.

I also gave myself grace. If I indulged in unhealthy foods for a few days, I lovingly let myself off the hook. I asked what I needed to support me in the moment, and if my heart said kindness and grace, I listened. Letting my IBSC beat me up when I was down only added to my stress, and I certainly didn't need more.

A few months later, when I dove into some work I needed to do as a parent to support my family, I found that it, and work on our family relationships, was a much easier focal point. I quickly dropped the focus I had on my own self-care. I noticed that my old patterns of prioritizing other people and things surfaced when I was exhausted and overwhelmed, so I needed to be much more intentional about taking care of myself. And asking others for help when I need it? Not my strength!

What living by heart looks like today is very different from twelve years ago when I got started on the journey.

Of course it is, love. Look at all the things that have changed. Look at all the progress you've made, my heart says, wrapping me in a warm embrace.

I am always a work in progress. I am always evolving, growing, and changing. Even if the stops along the train ride look familiar, I'm arriving at the station with different eyes and an evolved heart.

Whether you're dealing with stress, overwhelm, or are perhaps on the verge of burnout, it's important to prioritize your own self-care. Look at what stories you might be holding on to and whether nostalgia has rewritten your memory. Look at what's on your plate and whether it is serving or draining you. Let go of what doesn't serve you, wherever you can. Look at how you nourish and rest. What, if any, changes could you make to better fuel yourself for resilience?

Fear and Future Tripping

Do you ever find your thoughts spiraling out into the future?

Perhaps you worry about work and whether, when things are shifting around you, you might lose your job or your business as a result. Perhaps you worry about the health of a loved one, and if it gets worse, how that will affect them, you, and everyone around you. Or maybe you have other thoughts on your mind today that have you imagining the worst.

Alternatively, maybe you hit a recent homerun at work, and you imagine getting promoted as a result. Perhaps a loved one just received encouraging news about their health and you imagine them living a long, prosperous life.

The best description I've heard for what happens when our thoughts spin out into the future is "future tripping." It's a natural consequence of our minds having limited information, either positive or negative, and creating a future from that data that hasn't happened yet and may not happen.

The first time I heard the expression "future tripping," I didn't really understand it. What I did know was that I'd been spinning and swirling with fear-ridden thoughts for some time, and I wanted to get off the ride.

When my children were little, the biggest fears I had for them were whether they ate their lunch. Had I sent them to daycare with a change of clothes? Had they gotten enough sleep?

As they grew older, my ability to worry seemed to amplify, and my fears got bigger too.

Do they have friends? Are they "good" friends with positive in-fluence? Are they hanging with the "wrong" crowd? Are they okay at school? Will someone break their heart? Are they getting into cars with newly licensed teenage friends? Are they safe out there?

What I didn't understand was the impact my own "future trip-ping" was having on my experience with my kids, my experience in my marriage, and my experience trying to run a business on my own. I was too busy tripping about the future to be present in my life.

I came to understand "future tripping" by looking inward at what I was spinning, swirling, and spiraling about. The fear-ridden thoughts and what they were based on.

When my oldest son started dating in high school, he chose not to tell us about it. I remember feeling hurt when we finally met her and learned they'd been together for a few months already. I started future tripping.

"This is how it starts. He is distancing himself from us."
"He isn't going to tell me anything anymore."
"His girlfriend is more important to him than we are."

Looking back, it's easy to laugh at myself. How had I gotten there? What evidence, if any, made me start spinning out into the future? How could I possibly know what the future holds?

They were together for the next five years. And man, I future tripped a whole lot during those years:

"I hope she doesn't break his heart."
"How will he recover if they break up now?"
"He can't possibly stay with his high school girlfriend forever."

My tripping wasn't all doom and gloom. I also future tripped about positive futures:

"When they get married . . ."
"When they have kids of their own . . ."

All this projecting out into possible futures that hadn't happened yet stole my attention and focus away from the present. Instead of enjoying my son and our time together in the moment, I spent that time spiraling out into my head with worry and planning. And I missed out on what was right in front of me.

You might be asking, "Isn't this what we're supposed to DO as parents? Isn't it my job to be a 'mama bear' and protect my kids? Aren't I supposed to worry and plan so they don't have to?"

Certainly, society has told us that's what is expected of women. We're supposed to worry and plan and take care of everyone. But are we supposed to spend our time worrying and planning at the expense of joy and presence in our lives?

The energy invested in future tripping drains you and prevents you from accessing your full tank of innate resilience when you need it. Now, I'm not going to suggest that you don't worry. I certainly can't say that my work on reducing my own future tripping and strengthening my resilience has eliminated all worry. It hasn't.

But asking some key questions has helped me reduce the future tripping and wasted energy spent on things that may not even happen. It's helped me shift from my "mama bear" warrior into the compassionate warrior I want to be: the woman who pauses, assesses, and chooses when to rise and when to step back.

Here are a few of the questions that I ask myself when I catch myself future tripping:

"What am I really worried about? What's underneath this worry?"

"What information do I need to better understand this situation?"

"Who owns this problem?"

"Who owns this worry?"

"Is this something I can control or influence?"

"How is what I'm worried about helping me?"

"What can I let go of to be more present in this moment?"

Other questions I sometimes ask when I'm spiraling out with worry and fear are:

"What does my heart say about this worry?"

"How does this worry impact who I want to be?"

"Who can help me in this moment?"

I don't ask myself every question every time. And sometimes I start with the "who can help me?" question if I know I need some support to navigate the worry I'm trying to manage.

As you read the questions, which one or two stand out to you in this moment? Which question could be most helpful to you when you catch your thoughts spinning out into the future? Take a moment to write down the questions you feel could be most helpful to you.

Note that future tripping can impact your nervous system too. When your mind starts spiraling into the future, your body can experience the same kind of reactions that traumatic events can cause. Your thoughts create emotions based on your predictions of future events that haven't happened yet. As a result, you may want to include some of the activities in the "Resilience as a Practice" section to calm your nervous system before you use the reflection questions.

Recovering from the Spin

Now that you know what future tripping is, what can cause your mind to create future predictions and send you spinning out into the future, I invite you to reflect on the fears that may be keeping you stuck. Notice if you see any themes or patterns, as they may guide you to where to spend some extra time.

At fifty years old, I find myself reflecting a lot: on who I am now, who I think I've been, and who I want to be. One theme I found throughout my life was a sense of constant "striving." Wanting to be more, have more, and do more.

But I'm so very tired. I fell asleep on the couch recently at three in the afternoon. My judger self cackled with delight: *What's WRONG with you?*

I realized that despite all that I've learned on the journey, I am currently walking around in fear. I've let future tripping take over my thoughts, and my mind is spinning out of control.

NOTICE THE SPIN

Here are just a few of the future tripping thoughts currently racing through my mind:

- I'm afraid of never feeling comfortable again in my own skin, despite knowing that I can do it.
- I am afraid of failing at my business, despite running it successfully for eight years already.
- I am afraid that the recent changes in my health might be something serious, despite having no real evidence to support this fear.

Of course, at fifty, the health issues I've been struggling with could also be linked to menopause. By seeing my doctor, I could quickly address my concerns and possibly solve them swiftly with some hormone therapy. But somehow, I've rationalized that it's easier to not know, despite knowing how much mental strain future tripping places on me and depletes my resilience.

Have you ever chosen to ignore something big that is staring you right in the face? Perhaps there is something you are avoiding right now. How might future tripping be keeping you stuck?

NOTICE THE SIGNS

I can always tell when I am struggling. A few things happen:

First, I stop journaling for a week or two in a row. When I am not journaling, I am usually avoiding something or feeling so overwhelmed that I am not even making time to write.

Second, I notice that whenever I don't have a client call or a meeting scheduled, I move to the couch to "relax." There's no real reason for relaxing or needing to recover from something strenuous, yet it feels like I can't do anything that requires any kind of thinking or effort.

Third, I don't want to go anywhere, do anything, or see anyone. When I'm in this state and I get invited out, my immediate reaction is panic, followed by a swift decline. "No thanks, I'm busy." This is usually when the warning bells start ringing.

Noticing the warning signs can help you catch yourself before the mind spinning takes over. Once you catch it, you can then take steps to shift back to your heart.

So, what works to get me out of the future-tripping funk?

If I stay in judger mind, I will continue to beat myself up about it. My IBSC loves when I start spinning and listening to my judger self. The whole IBSC gets up and starts dancing. I hear their laughter, and my judger self says, *See, you haven't got a handle on this at all*. That doesn't help. In fact, it can send me spiraling further into the abyss.

RECOVERY

What works is leaning into my heart. I must get quiet, put my hand on my heart, take a few deep breaths, and listen. I ask her what she needs to tell me.

Rest, she whispers.

Oh, give me a break! That's all I've been doing, my judger self answers back.

Real rest.

I pause and take another deep breath.

Yes.

I feel the world around me slow down.

Another deep breath.

Yes, love. Like that.

You see, all the couch lounging isn't actual rest. I am binge-watching old shows and playing sudoku on my phone.

My brain is still spinning. I am not giving my mind, my heart, and my soul true rest.

One more deep breath.

Exactly.

My heart sees me. She *sees* me.

My head loves to judge me and make me feel like I'm not enough. But my heart sees me for who I am. And she loves me exactly as I am.

In this two-minute exchange, I shift from overwhelm to calm. It's almost impossible to believe it can happen that quickly. But it does. My nervous system calms right down, and I can feel a smile form on my face.

When I reflected on the two-minute exchange, I noticed that I hadn't connected to my heart in a few weeks. That's how I got here.

Connecting with my heart is a daily practice. When I do it daily, I keep myself on an even keel. Loving me. Letting love guide me. Leading from my heart instead of the noise and judgment in my head. Now, this isn't to abandon logic and rational thinking, it's to balance the scales so I am not guided solely by a mind that likes to create narratives that often aren't true or in my best interest.

My mind can lie to me way too easily.

My heart believes in me and has no agenda.

What are your thoughts on this heart-centered activity? How might it help you shift from spinning to still? From frenzied to focused? I invite you to take a pause, put your hand on your heart, take a few deep breaths and ask yourself, "What does my heart need right now?"

Music Fuels Resilience

Building resilience isn't about learning how to be resilient. You are born resilient. What you need to build instead are various tools to fuel that resilience. After you've done the work to eliminate the stories keeping you stuck, reduce the "comparison-itis" that drains you, and quiet the future tripping that sends you spinning, it's time to shift to focusing on fuel.

It's helpful to have a toolbox of fueling activities to draw upon. I've found that some work is better than other types depending on what challenge I'm facing, and the level of fuel I have in the tank starting off. For me, I discovered that music is one of the most powerful tools in my fueling toolbox, especially to shift my energy when I have limited time.

Music connects me to my heart almost instantly. And while I've loved music all my life, I didn't know it was a lifeline to my heart until I started doing some visualization work. It was through this work that my heart helped me make the connection between her and music.

For years, Saturday mornings were my favorite time of the week. On Saturdays, the kids slept in, but I'd still wake at dawn—my internal clock unable to shift from early rising on the other days of the week. The house was quiet, with only the soft sounds of breathing wafting down the hall from the rooms where my three sons slept. In those moments, it felt that all was right in the world.

One fine Saturday, on the spring equinox, the sun glistened on the bare limbs of the tree outside my window. The cloudless sky was a perfect blue that is unique to the sky alone. I felt the energy of the earth. I felt the increasing warmth of the sun. I paused to take a few deep breaths within the awesomeness of it all. In the silence, I felt deeply connected with my heart.

I should tell you that before I started this journey, I never enjoyed or appreciated quiet. I used to crave connection, and I always wanted to be engaged and in conversation with someone. The quiet used to make me feel isolated and alone with my thoughts and feelings. I didn't know how to be alone with myself. One of the many gifts of connecting with my heart, I now realize, is that I never feel alone anymore.

Once I started, I discovered that she's a deeper part of me that is a direct line to all the wonders of the universe. I had heard this idea many times before, of course, but I never really grasped it until I started connecting with my heart.

On that sunny Saturday morning, I closed my eyes and invited my heart to join me. I welcomed her with love, gratitude, and the deepest appreciation. I invited her to bring whatever I'm meant to share here with you.

I closed my eyes to receive her message. I felt the pages of my life turn as we traveled to the places I might explore. She stopped on a page; I couldn't quite make it out.

Trust me, she whispered.

I do.

I'm whisked to an open field. Tall grass is waving as the wind gently blows across the hills. The grass leans toward me as the wind touches my face. It is a kiss from Mother Earth as I'm invited to lie down in the softness. I stare up at the sparkling sun. I know I shouldn't look right at it, so I close my eyes to receive its warmth through my closed lids. They shine red and receive the glow openly. The sunlight dances with the tall grass as it brushes against my arms. The waving blades move between my closed eyes and the sun's rays. Shade, sun, shade, sun, shade, sun—the wind orchestrating their movement.

I can feel the wind, but I don't hear it. My ears are filled with music as I feed my mind with the complex, beautiful sounds of Led Zeppelin's fourth album. I'm fourteen years old, on vacation with my family, and it's the summer I discovered a new appreciation for music. The field is rich with red soil, the reddest soil I've ever seen. We're vacationing on Prince Edward Island, Canada's island province.

I lie in that open field for hours, listening to Robert Plant's voice crooning, soaking up every ounce of the sun's rays, and feeling the kisses of the wind.

The music held my hand and my heart as I rested my body and soul.

The sun sent his warmth and love to each weary bone, muscle, and vein.

The wind worked her magic through her gentle caress.

I was in complete contentment.

What I didn't recognize when I was fourteen was that I was healing myself through that practice. This was my first (albeit unconscious) healing session.

A few long-held stories begin to unravel with this memory.

While I believed I lost my heart when I was young, there she was in the field that day.

Even at fourteen, when I felt most alone and disconnected from the world. I can see now how she was there, how my heart spoke to me through music, through the sun, and through the wind. My heart was always with me. I was always worthy.

Yes, my love, she said to me as we returned to my bedroom on that Saturday morning.

"How can I bring these two parts of myself, my head and my heart, together?" I asked. "I feel like I have been struggling with this for so long." My heart then guides me to another memory.

It's early on a Monday morning when I arrive at the center. I spent twelve weeks a year running training programs at this center during my corporate years. It was my home away from home.

I say a quick warm hello to the staff at the front desk, then proceed to the room where I'll be leading a new group of wealth professionals for the next five days. As I walk in, the sun is shining through the wall of windows at the back of the room. I hang up my coat and change into the three-inch heels I facilitate in. These shoes make me feel awesome. They are leopard-patterned, soft to the touch, and I stand taller and straighter in them. It's amazing how a great pair of shoes can make you feel.

I am wearing my favorite red dress. It's such a rich red, slightly darker than cherry. The material feels like a cashmere sweater. It fits me exactly as it should. I run my hands across my hips. I feel beautiful.

My dress is sleeveless, so I also don a cross between a sweater and jacket. It is thin, black, and has a gorgeous cut to it that accentuates my figure. I feel like a goddess. Something is missing, though.

I cross to the table at the back of the room, feeling completely at ease in my body with each step. I connect my phone to the speaker, turn up the volume, and sing along with Led Zeppelin's "Fool in the Rain." I am fearless. I sing out without concern for who might be watching. I dance as I sing.

Participants for the program begin to arrive, and I wave them in as I continue singing and dancing. Some join in, others awkwardly beeline for a seat without making eye contact, and some leave to get a coffee. I don't feel fazed in the least. This is my moment when I am getting in the zone to lead this class. I'm in my happy place. The participants are wherever they are in their own journeys.

The song ends. I head back to the table to put on a curated playlist and turn down the volume to a more reasonable level. I approach the first participant sitting at a table and introduce myself. I am ready!

I leave this memory there and come back into my bedroom again. I feel a strong sense of something I'd known but hadn't acknowledged. I'd found harmony between my head and my heart in that training room. I'd already found a way to bring my corporate self and compassionate self together. So, why did it still feel like this was a battle to win?

I recalled how powerful and confident I'd felt in my body. *Yes, goddess.*

I recognized the importance of self-love and how my connection to my heart is a journey of self-love. *Yes, goddess.*

I discovered a few more insights from that one visualization:

I am most connected to the yin and yang of my own soul when I am facilitating. I noticed the distinct difference between facilitating in person and virtually. I realized how disconnected I'd been from that energy and the strength within myself during COVID. I still felt powerful and in tune with the participants when I facilitated virtually, but I wasn't as connected to my heart, my confidence, and my deep love of self as much in that medium. How curious!

I realized that I still needed to do more work to connect with love for myself physically. How was that blockage impacting other areas of my life and self too?

I am worthy.

Isn't it fascinating how all roads lead back here? Isn't it incredible how deep self-loathing can dig? So deeply that sometimes it isn't even visible until you start unraveling the stories?

What might you discover about yourself if you invited your heart to guide you? If the timing feels right, give yourself the gift of connecting with your heart. Put on a song that supports you. Place your hand on your heart, if that feels right for you. Close your eyes and ask her to share her wisdom with you.

Take a few moments to reflect after the song ends. Journal if that feels supportive. Notice what shows up. What might you be curious about and want to explore further?

I loved the power that music had in these two memories. I loved discovering that my heart was with me all along and she connected with me through music well before I listened to her directly. I loved how she used music to remind me that I've always been worthy.

Music is a source of strength that supports my resilience. It fuels me when my energy is low so I can access my innate resilience quickly when I need it.

By knowing how important music is to fuel me, I've curated different playlists to support me when I need to focus, when I need energy, or when I need calm. One of my favorite ones to listen to when I'm feeling stressed or overwhelmed is a "comfort and soothe" playlist with songs of hope, strength, and joy. Just listening to this playlist for ten minutes shifts me from worry to calm, anxiousness to peace. It is so powerful.

I encourage you to create your own energy-boosting playlist to support and fuel your resilience. Pick songs that give you energy and make you feel good. Test out songs and notice how they make you feel before you put them on your playlist. Create a list of ten songs to start, then add songs when you find ones that give you an energy boost. Most importantly, have fun curating your custom playlist.

Music can create energy, fuel your tank, connect you with your heart, and remind you of who you are at your best. Music is magic.

Here's a music mantra I use to express gratitude to my heart and to music. Feel free to use it or create your own mantra as part of your fueling resilience practice.

To my soul, heart, and mind.
To my Divine Self.
To my body.
To my worthiness.
To the music that connects all of me as one whole.
Thank you. Thank you. Thank you.
Love you. Love you. Love you.

Movement Fuels Resilience

In the earlier section on fear and future tripping, I mentioned how the body and especially your nervous system can get activated when you are stressed, overwhelmed, or feeling heavy emotions as the result of future tripping. There are many other situations and feelings that can activate your nervous system, but today, let's focus on the nervous system as it relates to resilience.

Many clients tell me the most effective tool they have to refuel is moving the body. Whether working out at the gym, running on the trails, or swimming in the lake, for many people, moving the body can quickly reduce anxiety and regulate the nervous system. Even if you aren't a fan of exercise, simply stretching the body, shaking out your limbs, or dancing in your chair can help.

I've struggled over the years to find a physical activity that brings me joy and doesn't hurt. For a short period of time, running was an outlet that worked for me, until it wasn't. I enjoyed cycling as a kid, but I didn't enjoy it when I tried to take it up as an adult. Walking is an activity I can do without pain, and it does bring me joy when I'm joined by someone, as long as the sidewalks aren't covered with snow or slick with ice. But I really wanted to find an activity I could do at home and at the cottage, all year round and on my own.

It's hard to look forward when the past feels brighter and more certain. It's easy to anchor to a memory. A moment or period when things seemed better, easier, and more controllable. Oh jeez, there's that dreaded word—control.

No matter what kind of saboteurs tend to get in my way, at the source is the matter of control. I like feeling in control. I try desperately to avoid feeling out of control. The things I think I can't control I may choose to abandon completely.

Exploring my need for control is uncomfortable. It's also helped me gain important insights on my journey.

On an Easter Sunday, I decided to try my very first somatic yoga workout. I declined an invitation to walk with my husband, kids, and the dogs, and chose to stay home to "work." Shortly after they left, I found myself curious about my choice. Why had I decided not to walk with them? Was it really about doing some work on Easter Sunday?

Or was it about something else?

As I sat reflecting, I realized I didn't want to go for a walk because I wasn't feeling good about myself. I wasn't feeling loved. I wasn't feeling energy. I was still in my pajamas. It was easier to say no than to say yes. If I stayed home, I'd stay in control.

My IBSC had a heyday:

You're overweight and you need to walk. What's wrong with you?!

You say you want quality time with your family, then you don't go with them. What's wrong with you?!

You're putting off the work you need to do anyway. What's wrong with you?!

I took a breath and invited my heart to guide me. "What does my heart want?"

Gently, she answered.

I'd heard that message before. It was subject to interpretation, so I needed more information.

"Gently for myself?"

Yes.

"Gently for others?"

Yes.

"Gently for the work?"

Yes. Yes, my love. Gently for all of it.

"Okay. Gently for all of it," I told myself as I walked through the house.

I felt hungry, so I wandered into the kitchen. Fresh, unopened bags of chips sat in plain view atop the refrigerator, tempting me. Instead of giving in, I turned toward the cupboard and grabbed a tall glass. I stood right in front of those chip bags as I filled my glass with water.

"I choose nourishment," I said out loud.

Yes, said my heart.

As I left the kitchen, I felt a small wave of energy. Okay, I'd missed the walk. What else could I do? Somatic yoga?

For weeks, somatic yoga had been showing up as a recommended activity on my Facebook feed. I didn't know what it was, but clearly the algorithm thought it was what I needed. Curious, I typed in "Somatic yoga day one" on Google. Lots of options appeared, but I let my heart choose one that felt good, a video on YouTube with a woman named Megan MacCarthy. Her voice was so gentle.

Gently.

Okay. I can do this. But I'd felt stuck and in pain for so long, I worried that I couldn't actually do it.

Gently, my heart whispered.

Okay. If I can be gentle with myself, maybe I can do this.

I let myself follow this gentle voice as she guided me through a body scan, then small movements, then larger ones. She encouraged me to "do what you can," and thirty minutes later I'd completed my first somatic yoga workout. I hadn't been able to do all the movements; my body was stiff, and some positions were really uncomfortable, but I chose to focus on *doing* it instead of judging how *well* I was doing it.

At the end of the workout, I was guided to do a final body scan to check in on how I felt after the workout compared to how I'd felt at the beginning. I noticed my body felt alive.

Yes, my heart whispered in delight. *Alive. Gently.*

I walked back into the kitchen and without a glance at the chip bags I refilled my water glass. Then I climbed the stairs to change out of my pajamas and get dressed.

With only thirty minutes of gentle movement, I felt connected and alive. My mind was cleared of the foggy haze. My body felt lighter and more relaxed. My heart sang with happiness. And the path ahead looked bright.

I found an activity I could do anywhere, at any time, and by myself. Somatic yoga made me feel good, released the tension in my body, regulated my nervous system, and cleared the fogginess in my head.

How can movement help you fuel your resilience? Maybe you already have a favorite activity or two that immediately comes to mind. If not, this is an opportunity to explore what types of move-ment work best for you. Test out new movement activities you're curious about. Reflect on past movement activities that used to bring you joy. Could they do so again? Explore whether you prefer activities alone or with others. Discover what movement activities fuel you, excite you, energize you, and bring you joy.

Resilience as a Practice

Let's highlight a few key concepts from this section on resilience. First, know that you are resilient. You were born resilient, so you don't need to get, grow, or build your resilience.

Having a resilience practice is about tapping into your existing resilience, removing old limiting beliefs that get in the way, and fueling yourself so you can access your own resilience when you need it most.

Rest and renewal aren't "nice to have" activities you can put off until the weekend or your next vacation. We're living in an uncertain, complex world and daily stressors are now the norm. You need to make time each day for activities that renew your energy and relieve you of some of the stress you're carrying. Hav-ing another cup of coffee won't help you replenish the depleted brain cells you lose from stress throughout the day.

You can't control the world around you, you can only control how you respond to it. That is resilience. It's how you bounce back when you're under stress, how you manage worry and fear, and how you face the world without needing to don your armor.

I recommend that you design your own practice with activities that best support you. It's important to build your resilience prac-tice slowly. Pick one area of focus at a time and take a week or two to integrate it before adding a new activity. Change takes time.

I know from my own experience that whenever I've tried to change too much in my routine at once, I get overwhelmed. I give up trying to change. Be kind to yourself and change just one thing at a time. Here are some ideas you may want to include in your own daily practice:

NOURISHMENT:

Explore the foods that give you energy and the foods that drain your energy. Understanding how food affects you and knowing what foods can improve or impede your resilience can be a game changer. For me, eliminating gluten and dairy from my diet helped increase my energy, reduce digestive issues, reduce the frequency of colds and flus, clear the brain fog, and balance my emotions. I also learned that drinking more water (nutritionists recommend consuming half your weight in ounces of water daily) helped reduce inflammation in my body, which reduced the physical pain I was experiencing. It also helped me sleep better at night. Take the time to learn about food, drinks, and your own body. While my heart guides my resilience, my body needs fuel to support it.

REST:

Rest is more than getting a good night's sleep. Rest includes breaks throughout the day to renew and refuel. Studies show that using down time to scroll on your phone increases hormones like dopamine and cortisol, which keep you in stress mode. So, the activities you choose to do throughout the day for rest need to reduce stress. A brief walk in the fresh air, petting an animal, or a quick five- to ten-minute catnap are some great ways to rest during your day.

Sleep is vitally important, not only for your resilience but also to allow your body to heal itself. During REM sleep, our minds process all the events of the day—it's like watching a movie of your day's events, and your body experiences it all a second time! If we don't get enough REM sleep, our minds don't process the events, and we carry everything into the next day. No wonder I sometimes feel so exhausted!

I need to have a consistent routine before bed that helps my body and my mind prepare for rest. When I don't follow my routine, I'll toss and turn for hours. When I follow my routine, I'm usually asleep within minutes of my head touching my pillow.

Experiment to figure out what the right amount of sleep is for you and the evening wind-down activities that best support your sleep. Test out different daytime activities that provide you with some rest throughout your day. Then build a routine into your daily practice for rest.

SILENCE:

Initially, I found sitting in silence uncomfortable. Now I know that sometimes finding moments of silence can help me shift from spinning to calm. Taking a pause and stepping away from the noise into a quiet space can be all I need to feel grounded and centered. Silence helps me connect with my heart and check in on what I may need to support me in that moment.

Perhaps there is a place in your home or at your work where you can go to find peace and quiet. This can be an effective tool to support you when you need to tap into your resilience.

MUSIC:

I shared a few examples of moments when music has really helped me connect with my heart, step into my power, and shift from overwhelm to calm. I've found in my coaching practice and workshop facilitation that music is an effective tool to change the energy or mood in the room.

You may already have a "go-to" song that you listen to when you need a boost. You may have a playlist or two that you've built to energize, focus, or work through your emotions. If not, take some time to play with the music you enjoy. Note which songs energize you, which songs calm you, which songs elicit an emotional response. Let your heart and your body guide you to curate your own playlist.

For me, when I need to focus, I want music without lyrics such as classical or meditation music. When I'm experiencing grief from losing my parents, I choose a playlist of songs from my childhood that connect me with my mom and dad. If you haven't explored how music could support you, I encourage you to try it out.

MEDITATION:

Research shows that meditation is an excellent practice for living mindfully. Since I've struggled with self-directed meditation, I prefer to use guided meditations through apps like Calm or Headspace to support me. I particularly like using the Calm app for bedtime meditations when I'm finding it hard to quiet the noise in my mind. I'll put on a thirty-minute sleep meditation and usually only remember the first ten minutes of it when I wake up the next morning!

You can also find some great guided meditations on YouTube if you don't want to purchase a meditation app. Test out what works best for you, and if meditating helps you clear your mind and connect with your heart, build it into your resilience practice.

BREATHING TECHNIQUES:

In Awareness, I shared an experience I had working with a breath-work practitioner. I also share a second guided breathwork experience in Trust. If guided breathwork interests you, there are some incredible breathwork practitioners who conduct breath-work classes if you want to use this powerful tool regularly to support you.

You can also learn some simple breathing techniques you can do yourself. What I love about having a few breathing techniques I know work for me is that I can use them anywhere, anytime, without needing a quiet space or technology to support me. My favorite breathing technique is called "box breathing." I picture a box in my mind while I box breathe for one to two minutes. Box breathing uses four equal counts of four. Breathe in for four, hold for four, breathe out for four, and hold for four.

Box breathing calms the nervous system, which allows you to shift from a feeling of anxiety or overwhelm into grounded, centered peace.

MOVEMENT:

Movement is a quick way to shift the nervous system from dys-regulated to regulated. Simple actions like stretching, shaking out your limbs, and dancing in your chair can release tension and activate the parasympathetic nervous system, which then relaxes you and can bring you a sense of calm. Daily practices like yoga, Pilates, and slow-moving martial arts like tai chi can help you renew your energy, maintain balance, and connect you to your resilience during the daily stressors in your life.

Sports, running, cycling, swimming and other aerobic activ-ities can help you release stress and tension. Additionally, they improve circulation, strength, and your energy, all of which help you keep your fuel tank full when you need it. If you already know the movement activities that work best for you, remember to use them regularly to keep you fueled. If you don't, have some fun testing out different movements and noticing which ones are most effective for you.

JOURNALING:

I know, I mention journaling in every section of this book. It's not an accident. Journaling is the best way to learn about yourself, identify patterns, and set intentions that lead to lasting change. Journaling while you test out the various tools and practices that can support you will help you identify what works best for you and what doesn't.

Here are a few questions you may consider while exploring your own resilience:

"What does resilience mean to me?"
"What does it feel like when I'm being resilient?"
"When have I felt most resilient?"
"When do I want to feel more resilient?"
"What helps me tap into my own resilience?"

Remember that different tools can work for different stressors and situations. Pay attention to what works best for you in which situations. Build out your fueling resilience toolbox, and trust that the resilience you're seeking is already within you. You were born resilient.

TRUST

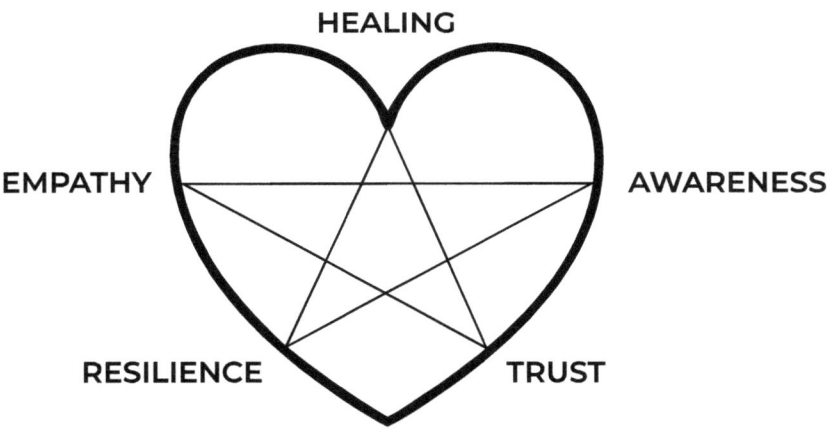

HEALING

EMPATHY   AWARENESS

RESILIENCE   TRUST

What Is Trust?

It's such a simple question, but does it have an easy answer? What is trust to you? How would you describe trust? What's important about trust to you? Give yourself a few minutes to think about what trust is and what it means to you. Notice how you feel as you think about it.

Picture a person you trust. What do you feel when you think about them? Where do you notice the feeling of trust in your body? What makes you trust them?

Now, think about someone you don't trust. Create an image of that person in your mind. What do you feel when you think about them? Where do you notice the feeling of distrust in your body? What makes you distrust them?

Take a moment to capture your thoughts on paper. What insights do you have about trust now? As you read through the Trust section of this book, keep those thoughts about what trust means to you in your mind. How does building trust support you in living by heart?

On my own journey, trust was the final practice I developed to support me in living by heart. Before I could learn to trust, I had to first heal the wounds I was carrying, build empathy for myself and others, dive deep into awareness to understand my ego and the parts of myself more fully, and fuel my resilience so I could navigate the rocky terrain of life. It was only after this work that I was ready to start building trust.

If you just opened this book and chose to start here at Trust first, you may experience some resistance within yourself as we dive into the work of building trust. If that happens, don't judge yourself. Resistance is a sign that some inner work is needed. Resistance can be a gift. You can notice it and thank it for giving you information.

Then, I invite you to pause, put your hand on your heart, and ask your heart where in the book you should go for support. Trust that your heart will guide you where you need to go in this moment. Turn to that section to work on the source of your resistance, then return to Trust when you're ready. Trust that your heart will tell you when it's time to return here.

Trust is a simple word to say but a difficult concept for most of us to describe. Trust is a feeling you have. You either trust someone, or you don't. There's no middle ground where you'd say, "I sort of trust them." It can be difficult to explain exactly why you trust someone, but it's usually easy to describe why you don't trust someone.

What about trusting yourself? Is it easy or hard? How do you know if you trust yourself? What happens if you don't trust yourself?

When I started doing my own work on trust, I believed I trusted myself completely, with my high control needs and warrior self fully developed. I discovered, though, that I didn't really trust myself, and my control needs and warrior were guards to protect me from that trust. I was surprised. I also didn't realize how important trust in myself was to embrace all I'd learned about living by heart. If I didn't trust myself, I couldn't share the insights I'd gained with other people. I certainly wouldn't write a book about it and be sharing the journey with you now.

During my coaching certification a few years later, I explored the importance of trust when making choices and committing to change. There are many types of trust, but I kept coming back to three critical types of trust that when embraced, can create powerful transformations, but if limited or nonexistent, prevent movement and growth.

As a coach, I talk to my clients about three types of trust: trust in self, trust in others, and trust in the process. We explore all three in our work together. And often, when a client has a block in the habits they want to change or the actions they wish to take, trust comes into the conversation.

Building a daily trust practice helps you know when trust is present or when you need to intentionally work on building more trust. I talk more about building your own trust practice at the end of this section, but for now, we'll focus on three simple questions:

- Do I trust myself?
- Do I trust others?
- Do I trust the process?

While writing this book, I did a lot of trust work. Whenever I'd get stuck, I'd pause to check in. I'd ask myself questions like "Am I starting this writing exercise in trust? Do I trust my heart to guide me? Do I trust the process?" If I wasn't feeling trust in myself or in the process, I used one of the tools I share in "Trust as a Practice."

So, how does trust impact Living by HEART? Living by heart is about bringing your whole self to everything you do, and that takes courage and vulnerability. You can't be vulnerable when you don't trust yourself or others that it's safe to put your whole self (your mind, heart, body, and soul) out there. You can't be courageous when you don't trust that the universe is with you on the journey. You can't trust all the parts of yourself until you know that your heart holds all parts of you with love and respect.

Learning to trust myself, trust others, and trust the process has been a journey for me. I'm still working on it, and like the other aspects of living by heart, it's something I practice daily. When I do trust myself, I feel freedom; I feel empowered. When I trust others, I feel supported and connected. When I trust the process, I feel joy and peace.

Trust in Self

Do you trust yourself? If you aren't sure, that's totally normal. Exploring trust in yourself can take time, and you may find that your answer changes depending on the context of the situation you're in and how you're feeling in that moment.

Do I trust myself? Sometimes. Strange, isn't it? That I should trust myself sometimes and not at others?

When do I tend to trust myself? I tend to trust myself when I am doing something I love and am passionate about. When I stop thinking so much and get out of my own way. For example, I feel complete trust when I am facilitating workshops. I feel complete trust when I am coaching my clients. I feel complete trust when I am singing.

Sometimes, trust comes after I start doing something. When I take the first run on the ski slope in the morning, for example. I'm timid, and I don't trust myself or my body to safely transport me to the base of the hill. I wait and allow others to ski ahead of me. I notice my body feeling rigid, my muscles stiff. As I push off slowly over the edge of the hill, my heart races and I worry I won't make it. Then I plant my pole, and my skis make their first awkward turn in the snow. The next turn comes a little easier, and the third smoother still. By the time I reach the bottom of that first run, I feel the trust in myself return.

I notice that on the ski hill, the trust in myself can come and go if I let my ego get in the way. My ego worries: "How do I look out here? What do others think of my skiing? Did anyone see my ski catch on that last turn?"

When I bring myself back to my heart, I feel alive and whole. I feel freedom, and the fresh air takes over. I know that my body knows how to ski, and I trust it. I trust my body to navigate the terrain and handle whatever bumps appear on the path. Skiing is a beautiful capturing of the shift between my ego and my heart, between inner critic and inner ally—you've got this.

Take a few minutes now to reflect on your own thoughts about trust in yourself. Capture your thoughts on paper if you want to. Writing down your thoughts can help you see patterns in your thinking and help you build trust in yourself.

Once I started working on building trust in myself and trusting my heart to guide me, I began receiving guidance from within that helped me shift from stuck into action. Here's just one example of guidance I received while I was writing this book. As you read it, consider how tuning in and trusting your own inner wisdom might support you when you get stuck.

TRUST IN SELF: PCC AND THE "AHA"

Recently, during a "soul connections" call with a fellow coach, I had an aha moment that felt transformational. Then a "Leading with Heart" video I created on March 16, 2020, appeared in my feed. As I watched the video, I realized that I am relearning things I used to know. But rather than sit in judgment about it, I chose to embrace the love-led lens of calm curiosity and, in the words of Benjamin and Rosamund Zander, say, "How fascinating!"

On the call, I told my fellow coach about my struggle to complete my PCC, my Professional Certified Coach credential. I'd completed the five hundred hours of coaching required to apply for the credential more than five years ago. So, what's the issue?

To apply for the PCC, I need to submit two recorded coaching calls for evaluation to ensure I meet the core coaching competencies. And I have a big mental block about it. I have received coaching from numerous seasoned coaches to overcome this block. I have explored it ad nauseum. Just thinking about exploring it further mentally exhausts me. I just can't do it.

So, after years of trying to understand the mental block, I've reached the conclusion that I just need to "get that sh*t done." I need to push through the fear and do it anyway. I know, it sounds a little Tony Robbins-esque. But sometimes for me, it's the only way to get through it. I won't feel better about it until it's over.

My coaching friend asked if we could talk about it. I felt resistance but agreed.

I don't know whether it was my heart's curiosity or my judger's exhaustion that answered her. She shared that from her perspective, she didn't see me showing up as my usual self when I spoke about this PCC dilemma.

"Hmm. That's interesting. Say a little more about that," I said, encouraging her.

After a bit of back and forth, she asked me, "After all the coaching and exploration you've already done, could there be an ingredient you're missing?"

Oh boy. That question hit a nerve! I felt myself feeling resistance and anger. *Hello, Anger ball!*

How dare my friend even suggest that I might have "missed" something! My insides were screaming. My judger self activated, and my warrior self got ready to fight. I sat for a moment and let the question reverberate through me.

I held back the internal army, put my hand on my heart, and channeled curiosity. "What do you mean?" I asked.

"Well, I don't want to give the words to it, but I wonder about compassion and forgiveness, and whether you, like me, struggle to give yourself those things."

My eyes instantly welled with tears, the internal army washed away by a wave of emotion. Oh, sweet lord, there's something here, isn't there?

Yes, my love, my heart answered.

I looked up to the ceiling, trying to keep the tears in my eyes, but a few escaped down my cheeks. I pushed my glasses up on my forehead to wipe my face, then let out a long sigh. "Damn, you're good," I said to her and smiled.

In that moment, I realized that while I do practice compassion daily, I hadn't applied it to this specific issue. I am also still learning self-forgiveness.

We chatted a few minutes more about learning and trauma and how to help clients connect with the pain they are holding that's preventing them from moving forward.

I talked about how when people are activated and caught up in their stories, we, as coaches, can support them in shifting to calm, conscious, and curious. As I spoke, I felt the shift happen instantly within myself. I realized something I hadn't been aware of before.

When it came to completing my PCC, I'd been carrying around this story of "can't finish it" and the reasons why, for so long, I hadn't realized how activated my nervous system was when I talked about it. I didn't realize that I'd left my heart-centered self and traveled into the headiness and anxiety of my mind.

My whole body was responding to a heightened frequency of frenetic energy. I was talking faster, with more judgment and certainty, and I was on fire in a way that prevented presence and focus. My "just do it" energy was so vastly different from living by heart. And I didn't know I was in that state at all because it had become normal.

Then, sitting in the calm, curious, heart-centered space, I felt completely different about my PCC dilemma and toward the stories I had been holding around it. Wow! I expressed this new awareness to my friend and thanked her.

In knowing that this moment was just one small step toward reclaiming my love for myself, I felt excited and empowered. This was a moment I wanted to capture to come back to in the months ahead, so I took time to journal about what I learned about shifting from "just do it" energy to my heart-centered energy that I could trust to support me.

In viewing my video series "Leading with Heart" that I recorded just two days into the COVID-19 lockdown in Ontario, Canada, I was struck by my own insights and awareness so clearly present on that day—insights and awareness that I've felt so incredibly disconnected from over the past few years.

The topic on the video I watched was shifting from head to heart. I almost laughed aloud when it started. I love how the universe gives you exactly what you need when you need it. After the conversation with my coach, it was no accident that this memory appeared in this moment.

In this video, I talked about three key concepts:

1. Connect with your heart. Notice if you are living in the frenetic headiness of facts and thoughts and place a hand on your heart to shift into the heart space. Notice how your breathing slows down and the rate of speech does too. The heart is the calm, curious brain within us.

2. Bring empathy. This isn't about emotional intelligence, it is emotional embodiment. It is connecting with the love, care, and compassion for ourselves and others so we can validate emotions and support each other from a place of genuine love.

3. Practice gratitude. Gratitude can shift us from the anxiety of uncertainty into a place of seeing what is beautiful in the world, what we have versus what we don't. We can zoom out to see what's beyond the moment of stress and zoom in to see what we already have within us.

I don't quite know how the pieces of the journey are going to come together yet, but I am trusting in myself and my deeper knowing, trusting the process of writing every day, and trusting in the universe to give guidance and send messages as I need to receive them.

When I reflected on the experience, I noticed I was not only *not* trusting myself, but I'd fixated on a belief about not being able to finish my PCC that was keeping me stuck. If I'd checked in with my heart sooner, I might have seen the story and shifted my energy. I hadn't trusted myself to work through it. Then, the universe reminded me that I already had all the tools I needed within me. Have I mentioned that the universe has a great sense of humor?

Take a moment to pause and put your hand on your heart. Close your eyes if you want to, or if you leave your eyes open, try to stare at one spot in the room and soften your gaze. Take a few deep breaths and ask yourself one question: What if I trusted myself more?

TRUST IN SELF: LISTENING TO YOUR HEART

I know that I talk a lot in this book about listening to your heart. At its roots, Living by HEART is all about bringing your head and your heart together and turning up the volume on your heart. Trusting that she's with you. Trusting that she brings wisdom. Trusting that your heart won't let you down and will love you no matter what.

When I first started on this journey, I longed to be at the end of it right away. My warrior self just wanted the fight to be over. My IBSC loved to party when I stumbled along the way, so I wanted that to stop, and I wanted my heart to speak to me whenever I demanded her to. Hello, Warrior self.

I was impatient. I needed to learn to live in the present moment and trust that my heart was with me, even when I couldn't hear her.

When I ask myself, "What does my heart say?" sometimes I can access her instantly and receive a message from her. Other times I feel my head scanning, searching to connect with her. This used to really frustrate me.

"What's wrong with me?" I'd ask. *Hello, Judger self.*
"Why can't I do this more easily?"

The more frustrated I got, the more impossible it seemed to reach my heart. Imagine trying to grasp a rope that is just out of reach, and the harder you strain, the farther you extend your arm, the farther the rope moves away.

I'd stomp my feet, pout, and cross my arms.

"Humph," I'd mumble. I'd act like a four-year-old child. Then, when I'd give up in defeat, I'd hear her.

Yes, my love.

It took me a long time to realize that I couldn't force my heart to answer. She flows like water. She answers when she's ready, at her own pace and in her own time. She can't be rushed. She's calm, cool, and curious. My heart answers when I get quiet and present. She shows up when I stop trying so hard.

Now, when I ask my heart for guidance, I trust she will provide it when I am ready to receive it. And she does.

Here's what my heart wanted me to share with you:

- You can't see what lies ahead. You can't "know" the future.
- You can set your intentions based on what you know and can see now.
- You can have gratitude for where you are today.

- You can believe that the universe works with you and for you.
- You can believe that things happen for you, even if you can't see the growth and learning from it in the moment.

Challenges and barriers before you direct you to other great opportunities you cannot yet see. Each step you take, each pause you embrace to soak up the magic around you, each moment of connection . . . these are gifts in your life. Not what's "out there," but what's right here. Now. You can trust in yourself and in your heart.

So, slow down and breathe. Get quiet and present. Turn off all distractions and sit with yourself in the silence. This is where your heart lives.

Trust in Others

Do you trust others? You may want to refer to the questions you asked yourself in "What Is Trust?" What does trust mean to you? What feelings do you have when you think about someone you trust? When you think about someone you don't trust?

Some clients I work with trust people too much. Other clients don't trust people enough. Consider your trust in others like a scale where zero is absolutely no trust and ten is complete trust. How would you rate yourself on that scale right now?

There is no wrong answer. Let this exploration be a judgment-free zone. No matter where you are on the scale of trusting others, you are exactly where you're meant to be in this moment. This is for your information only, and what you choose to do with the information is up to you.

For me, exploring and expanding my trust in others was an uncomfortable process. The warrior in me believed the only person I could trust and depend on was myself. Just thinking about trusting others made me feel exposed and vulnerable. My IBSC danced with delight!

On the "trusting others" scale, I started out at a two, and I gave myself a two instead of a zero because I did trust professionals in my life (like my doctor, lawyer, and accountant). I also cautiously trusted some broader institutions, so I didn't feel like I could say I was at zero. But it's fair to say that my trust in others was very low. It felt risky to change it. But my heart knew that to live authentically as my whole self, I needed to learn to trust others.

Once you know where you are on the scale, you can choose where you want to go from there. If your score is low, you might start with a question like "What's important for me about building trust in others?" If your score is high, you might ask yourself, "What would be different if I was more mindful about who and when I trusted others?"

Take a moment to reflect on your current score on the "trusting others" scale. What does this score mean to you? If your judger self shows up while you are reflecting, invite her to go play on the swings for a while, then put your hand on your heart. Take a few deep breaths. What does your heart say about your score? What's important for you to think about right now?

I'm not suggesting that you put blind trust in everyone. That isn't the goal. Living by HEART is about mindfully and intentionally building trust in others. It's seeing where distrust may be getting in the way of building meaningful relationships in your life, where distrust may be getting in the way of you living your purpose and leading in your career or in your community. It's about building trust in others so you can live authentically.

By knowing that I'm a work in progress, my journey to building trust in others hasn't been easy, nor has it been in a straight line—it's been curvy, with ups and downs and a lot of learning and reflecting. I know I've made progress.

Do I trust others today? Sometimes. More than trusting others, I've embraced this deep belief that people are doing the best they can with where they are at in the moment.

I hear a soft chuckle. *That is trust, my love.*

Yes, I suppose it is. I trust that people do the best they can with where they are at. This has helped me greatly in relating to others, having empathy and compassion, and accepting that others are not here to deliver the outcomes I want or expect but to be the best versions of themselves they can be in that moment.

I cannot tell you how much understanding and embracing this belief has supported me throughout the last five years—with family, friends, colleagues, and clients. It has helped me remove the pedestal and the hierarchical way our minds have been trained to think.

There is no one above me or below me. We are all humans on an even playing field, all doing our best with what we have and where we're at right now.

TRUST IN OTHERS: BREAKING DOWN ROADBLOCKS

Let me share one of the greatest challenges I had in learning to trust others. As you read it, look for the insights that might apply for your own journey into mindfully trusting others.

The hardest challenge for me to overcome when learning to trust others was relinquishing control. I'd depended on myself because I believed that only I could deliver results at the standard I expected. If I trusted someone else, they wouldn't do it to the standard I'd set. And numerous past experiences validated that limiting belief.

It was painful to see myself this way and admit it out loud. Even with all the awareness work and my understanding of my ego, this challenge continued to show up when I began working on trust. The IBSC cheered and gloated when they had a chance to berate me again.

See, you'll never be able to trust anyone else. Why even bother? my judger self said, kicking off the attack.

Lots of better coaches than you partner easily and bring on people to help them grow. You'll always play small, my comparison self said, chiming in.

You just work better alone. You're a fighter. You don't need anyone else, my warrior self stated with absolute certainty.

I struggled to turn down the volume on my IBSC and to tune into my heart. I really doubted that I could change and trust to let others in.

What might be possible if you did? my heart asked.

I thought about my heart's invitation. What if I focused on curiosity over criticism? What might be possible?

During my coaching certification, I was fortunate to connect with three incredible women who were also on the journey to become certified professional coaches. We talked about how we wanted to support women, especially women leaders, and the difference we wanted to make in the world. Through those connections and as we each launched our own coaching practices, an idea began to take shape.

Together, we could bring the best of ourselves to a women's weekend retreat. When we dreamed and visualized this event together, it was magical. When we decided to commit, book the location, build the workshop, and invite the women, I was forced to face the tough truths about my difficulty trusting others.

Sometimes, my warrior self jumped in to take charge, creating friction with the team. Other times, when I felt judged or undervalued, my IBSC took over, and I'd check out of discussions, putting my walls up to protect me. While I was passionate about the purpose of our work and loved the women on the team, I really struggled to manage myself and show up as the authentic whole self I wanted to be.

We ran two weekend retreats before our foursome disbanded. I knew I had to do some difficult and uncomfortable inner work on my trust in others, my ego and my control needs, and the limiting beliefs that were keeping me stuck.

One of these fellow coaches and I were still dreaming together. We decided to build a group coaching program for women leaders, and in January 2020, we ran our first Women.Lead. Now. workshop. I still struggled with relinquishing control and managing my warrior self and the IBSC, but I'd done some inner work and wanted to learn to trust others more.

Over the next four years, we ran eight group coaching leadership programs for women leaders across Canada. The work was so rewarding! The growth in building my trust in others was a beautiful bonus.

Together, we learned how to communicate when one or both of us were stuck. Our desire to work together was greater than my warrior self and IBSC, and I learned how to draw upon my heart when I felt myself struggling to self-manage my ego and my emotions. I learned to let my partner run things her way, trusting that she would do a great job and that there was more than one way to accomplish something. Did I stumble along the way? Absolutely! But believing that she was doing the best she could, believing that she cared about me and about our work together, helped me shift when I got stuck.

I'm so grateful she was willing to walk that journey with me and hold space for me to learn by doing, which, ultimately, is truly the only way to learn, grow, and change.

While this is a work-related story, the challenges of working with others and trusting them applies to all aspects of your life. How did you relate to this story? What insights do you take away from it? Take a moment to capture some of your thoughts.

TRUST IN OTHERS: GETTING FEEDBACK

Trusting others isn't just seeing other people at their best, it is also about receiving from others openly. As a coach, I notice that often clients receive incredibly positive feedback from others, yet they don't believe it. What would happen if you could see yourself through someone else's eyes?

I am naturally my own worst critic, and I suspect you are too. It can be difficult to consider seeing yourself differently from the stories you've been telling yourself for years.

If you've ever asked for feedback or testimonials from other people, you'll know the courage it takes to trust others when making such a request.

I remember the first time I put out a public request for others to reflect on how they see me. Just the idea of making such a request made my stomach churn and a gigantic lump form in my throat. I was certain I would throw up.

As I typed the words for the request I planned to post on Facebook, my hands trembled.

I wrote, rewrote, deleted. Started again. Was I really going to ask the public for the words they would use to best describe me? Could I really be so vulnerable?

I worried about what people would say. Then I worried that no one would respond. You know that fear, right? The fear that you will put out a request and not receive a single comment or "like"? The IBSC loved taking that fear and blowing it up like a balloon.

Who are you to ask people for feedback?
Do you really think anyone actually cares about you?
No one even thinks about you.
Only true influencers get engagement on Facebook.

The IBSC's dance party ensued. They delighted in making my fear bigger and the hole I was falling into deeper.

Gentle, my love, my heart whispered. *Just let yourself come back to center.*

I took a deep breath and went back to the post and my request for insight. The only way for me to see myself through others' eyes was to ask them. I couldn't make assumptions. Despite my strong sensation of nausea mixed with fear, I copied the text and pasted it into Facebook. Without reviewing it, I immediately pushed "publish" and left the app.

I noticed the sensations in my body shift. In addition to the nausea I was experiencing, my heart started racing. It thumped in my chest like it was trying to escape. I wondered whether I should delete the post. To prevent myself from pulling it down, I decided to take a walk.

The best way to calm my nervous system once activated is getting outside, and on that day, I knew I needed to remove myself from my phone, the room, and the entire house so I could release the pent-up fear within me. So, I walked out the door. Down the steps. Out onto the sidewalk. The fresh air invited me to take some deep cleansing breaths. Breathe in. Breathe out. Breathe in loving energy. Breathe out the fear within me.

By the time I reached the end of the first block, I felt calmer. By the second block, I knew that no matter what happened with my post, I would be okay. I was safe. I was worthy. No comments from the outside world could change that.

When I returned home thirty minutes later, I took another deep breath and checked Facebook. There were twenty-one comments on my posted request for feedback, plus a few private messages. People showed up to support me and provide the insights I was looking for. And more comments and insights followed over the next few days.

I noticed how little trust I'd had in others when I was preparing to make the request. I noticed how my IBSC tried to derail me and keep me stuck with limiting beliefs, self-doubt, and fear. I also noticed how my heart helped me detach from the outcome. She reminded me that no matter what happened, I would be okay.

What did you experience reading this story? What insights can you apply to your own trust in others? What's the takeaway for you? Take a moment to reflect and write down any thoughts that might support your work on trust in others.

Trust the Process

Do you trust the process? Your first response to this question might be asking a question: What process?

It could be any process you are taking part in. Trusting the process requires faith that even though you can't see the end or know exactly when you'll reach it, you'll get there. For example, reading this book and the work you're doing to bring your head and heart together is a process. Choosing to do the activities and respond to the prompts is trusting the process.

When you start something new, it can be helpful to ask yourself, "Do I trust the process?" If the answer is yes, you're ready to proceed. If the answer is no, you may want to ask yourself some additional questions: "What do I need to support me? What could help me trust the process? What might I need to let go of?"

Your trust in the process along the way can change. You may start a process fully open and ready to embrace the unknown, then get stuck when you aren't getting the results you hoped for when you wanted them. Checking in throughout the process can help you shift from being stuck to going with the flow of the current again.

Do I trust the process?

It feels funny asking myself this question while writing this book. My answer depends on whether I'm answering as a coach or as a client.

When I first start working with a new client, I invite them to trust the process of coaching. I tell them that change is not an event, it occurs over time. Throughout our work together, when they get frustrated with their progress or places where they get stuck, I remind them that coaching unfolds through a series of conversations and actions they put in place. At the end of the coaching engagement, we look back on the journey, the steps they took along the way, and the growth they experienced to get to where they are now. Then we celebrate their progress and how they trusted the process.

As a client, both personally and professionally, the warrior in me is impatient. She wants results now, and if she doesn't see them, she pushes me to move on. My heart knows and believes in the process. She's patient and willing to wait, trusting that change will come when it's time. My heart isn't attached to outcomes.

After decades of having my warrior leading the charge, it's been difficult to shift from being results-oriented to focusing on my intentions. It's been difficult to trust a process I can't see and believe that change will happen over time. That's not how I'm used to operating.

Think about driving a car on your life's journey. Is your warrior used to sitting in the driver's seat? Or does another part of you normally drive? Which part of you would be most helpful for you to trust the process? What would happen if you let your heart drive?

Give yourself time to think about these questions. Notice if your warrior is pushing you to keep reading instead of taking time to embrace and trust the process. What might be possible if you slowed down and gave yourself some space to reflect and learn about who's driving your car right now?

TRUST THE PROCESS: LEARNING TO LET GO

Take a pause before reading the next story to reflect on what processes are underway in your life right now. Do you trust them? Are you giving them space to breathe and expand? Consider where you are now and check in at the end of this story to see where you are after it.

In November 2023, I joined a women's business-owner mastermind group. Two incredible women I adored, Rachel and Alyssa, were running this virtual mastermind, and after engaging in a few different programs with them, my heart craved the connection, learning, and inspiration I knew would come from joining the group.

The beauty of a virtual mastermind group is that one can choose how involved they want to be. Join the weekly meeting live or watch it on the replay? Camera on or camera off? Speak up or quietly observe? I liked the flexibility of joining the sessions on my own terms. It also meant that I could choose to hide if I wanted to.

Sometimes, having the freedom to choose isn't good for me. When in a state of overwhelm, I tend to shut down and hide. COVID restrictions made this easier for me. Once the restrictions were lifted, however, I found it hard to engage in social activities when feeling low.

Rachel mentioned on one of the calls that they were organizing an in-person, one-day retreat for anyone in the mastermind who wanted to attend.

My heart danced with delight. *Yes!*

My IBSC all started speaking at once: *You can't possibly go. If they meet you in person, they won't like you as much. It's too long a drive to get there. If you sign up and then change your mind, you'll be wasting money.*

But my IBSC had kept me from so many events already. I was tired of listening to them. I knew it was time to listen to my heart. As soon as the registration for the retreat opened, I signed up. The IBSC continued with their chatter, trying to discourage me. I thanked them and hushed them. My heart leapt.

In June 2024, the sun shone brightly in the clear blue sky as I got myself ready to attend my first in-person retreat with the mastermind group. I didn't know what to wear to this event, and I wanted to feel great in my skin.

You can still cancel, taunted my judger self.

No matter what you choose to wear, the other women will look better than you, said my comparison self.

It doesn't matter what you wear, whispered my heart. *Just be you.*

So, I stepped into some work clothes I felt good in, then put on my favorite necklace, a beautiful set of wings in gemstone tones I'd purchased in Nosara, Costa Rica, during our last trip there. I call this necklace my "Wonder Woman" necklace because I feel like an empowered Amazon woman when I wear it. Finally, I threw on a little makeup to freshen up my face, jumped in my car, and got on the road.

Driving to the retreat, I listened to my favorite "women's conference" playlist I'd curated back in 2013 for a conference I'd hosted. I sang along with each song, feeling more and more aligned with my heart. More and more alive.

I arrived at the retreat early, so early that the hosts were still getting the room ready, so I waited in my car. My IBSC started to raise their voices, warning me that I should just leave and that I wouldn't fit in with the young, fit, energetic moms, many of whom were half my age.

Trust, my love, said my heart. *They love you already.*

When I noticed a few other women leaving their cars to enter the retreat, I slowly walked toward the entrance, feeling nervous about meeting these incredible women in person. At the door, Rachel and Alyssa greeted me with huge warm hugs and overflowing excitement to finally meet me in person. I felt my eyes brim with tears.

As I entered the room, another woman from the mastermind group approached me, hugged me, then looked at my necklace. "Your necklace is beautiful. It's from Bloom, right?" she said, with more of a statement than a question.

"Yes, it is," I said with surprise and a smile.

"I have a necklace from there too, although mine is quite different. Their stuff is so amazing."

Now, I've long believed in the magic of the universe. This moment really blew me away, though; Nosara is a tiny town on the Pacific coast of Costa Rica, and Bloom is a bohemian boutique that only sells their handcrafted jewelry from that one location. What were the chances that at a small women's retreat at a café in Puslinch, Ontario, I'd meet a woman who knew exactly where my necklace was from?

These brief interactions sent my IBSC into the trunk of my car, and my heart sat proudly beside me as my wingwoman. *Yes, love. Take it all in!*

The morning flew by faster than I wanted it to. I felt so connected, supported, and loved by this group of spectacular women. I didn't want it to end. It was hard to believe that just a few hours earlier I'd debated canceling and staying home.

I'd only planned to stay for the morning activities and then drive home after lunch. Rachel and Alyssa encouraged me to attend a breathwork session before I left. I said I'd see if I could swing it.

As I got in my car, I debated whether I should just get on the road or drive over to the lake to do the breathwork session. I had a long drive home ahead of me, and an even longer drive to the cottage after that. Did I really have time for breathwork?

The morning at the retreat was better than I'd anticipated, and I wasn't quite ready to leave it yet. I wanted to spend some more time with these women.

I checked in with my heart. Should I drive home now or stay?

Stay, she whispered.

So, even though I wasn't properly dressed for a breathwork session . . .

Even though I hadn't brought a yoga mat . . .

Even though I was hot and tired . . .

Even though it would be better to just get on the road . . . I drove over to the lake instead.

Sometimes you must trust the process.

Most of the women had already found their space and placed their mats on the large dock overlooking a gorgeous lake. I stood awkwardly at the back of the dock and watched every-one else chat.

See, said my judger self. *You should have left when you planned to.*

Everyone else is dressed for this and you're not, said my comparison self.

Just breathe, said my heart.

As I took a deep breath, one of our retreat hosts came over to me and pointed to the mat at the edge of the dock, right in front of the instructor. "That's for you," she said with a smile.

There was no getting out of it now and there was no hiding at the back. I was committed.

The breathwork instructor asked who had done breathwork before, and I put up my hand. Thinking about it reminded me of how emotional I'd been during my first breathwork session. Instantly, my eyes welled with tears. *Uh-oh. This is not a good start.*

Then I heard my heart answer: *Yes, love. It's exactly what you need right now. It is the perfect way to start.*

I was self-conscious about my body, what I was wearing, and how I looked lying there on the dock. I kept my legs bent with my sock-covered feet firmly planted on the mat. I tried desperately to ground myself.

My hands rested instinctively on my belly just below my belly button—my "lower dantian," as we referred to it in my Tao Hands practice. Before the breathwork began, I started taking some deep cleansing breaths into my lower dantian and visualizing a ball of light forming there.

The instructor played some beautiful music for us to breathe with. The sun shone brightly, and there was a soft breeze blowing in from the lake. I could hear the water gently lapping the shore. I realized in that moment that I had never done work like this outside and marveled at how magical it felt. *I must start doing meditation, yoga, and breathwork outside when I move to the cottage this summer.*

Then the breathing exercises began. So, too, did the emotions. The first thing I noticed was just how long it had been since I took a truly deep breath. I realized that for the past year and a half, maybe even longer, I'd been "shallow breathing." The stress and fear I'd faced since the challenges in our family began left me barely catching my breath.

Just the feeling of my lungs filling fully with air felt safer than I'd felt in months. The universe and love enveloped me. I let out a soft sob. The tears rolled steadily.

As I took in the next deep breath, I also noticed that I'd spent a year watching my son sleeping. Making sure he was still breathing. Terrified of walking in and seeing him cold, no longer taking breath. I realized how each breath I witnessed gave me both a brief sense of relief and a sense of terror that this could go on forever.

Bigger tears spilled out and down into my ears. It was hard to keep with the breathing pattern as I sucked in air between my sobs. Then, at just the perfect moment, the instructor placed her hands on the tops of my feet and held them. I don't know how long she was there, but her touch grounded me and freed me at the same time.

I focused on the music, the melodic voice of our incredible instructor, and the sounds of the water. I came back into my body for a moment. The intensity slowed and I caught my breath. I placed my left hand on my heart and kept my right hand on my belly. I could feel the energy moving between my heart and my gut, the ball of light filling all the space between them as if they were one. And then I felt an intense ache.

I missed my mom. Oh, how I wished my mom were there. I wished I could hug her and talk to her, hear her voice and receive her words of love and encouragement. My sobs increased again, the tears flowing freely.

Suddenly I felt a hand on my left shoulder. I knew it was the instructor's hand, but how had she known? The way she placed her hand on my shoulder. The shoulder she chose, the placement of her hand—it was exactly how Mom had touched my shoulder. Lovingly.

And while the contact wasn't from Mom, I knew it was a message from her. I knew she was with me. I felt her presence and her love hold me close. I let all the emotions within me that I had been trying to contain fully release.

Floods of tears and loud sobs.
Letting it all out.
Letting it all flow out of me.
No longer contained or constricted.

There were fifteen other women on that dock that day, but I wasn't aware of any of them. This breathwork session took me exactly where I needed to go and helped me release from all the pain, worry, fear, stress, and tension I had been carrying. I was free.

As the instructor slowly brought us back to the dock and back into our bodies, I continued to let the tears run down my cheeks. When I opened my eyes, I wiped my face a little, even though I knew I was safe and didn't need to hide anything. What a remarkable group of women. What an incredible experience. I was so glad I had stayed.

Our hosts and the instructor encouraged me to take some time to settle and reflect before jumping in the car for the long drive home. I was emotionally drained, yet I felt more alive than I'd had in months. I felt so much lighter.

Before I left, the instructor and I had a long hug. I thanked her for the incredible gift she'd given me. I don't think I had the words to adequately express all that had transpired. I told her about the touch on my shoulder and receiving the message from my mom even though I knew she didn't need an explanation. I cried as she nodded and hugged me again. She intuitively knew when to touch me and where to make contact.

I made my rounds to give hugs and say my goodbyes to all the women with whom I'd had the pleasure of spending my day. We took some photos. Then I hugged the retreat hosts and headed toward my car.

This day, this breathwork session, this release.
Gifts I would remember for years to come.
My heart was full.
Trust the process.

Take a moment to reflect on where you are now. What, if anything, changed from before you read this story to now? What insights can you take away?

Capture your thoughts in your journal. Look back at the notes you've made so far on Trust. Notice if you see any patterns between trusting yourself, trusting others, and trusting the process.

CHERISHING MOMENTS

Do you do a yearly reflection? Do you take time to look back and look forward? What do you do with the insights you learn?

Many people take time over the weeks leading up to year end to look back and review their year. For a number of years, I've sent a reflection sheet out to my past and present clients, encouraging them to conduct a review of their past year and set intentions for the upcoming one. What I didn't realize, however, was that this activity can be done with either your judger self or your heart. Which part of you leads the reflection can dramatically change both the experience during your reflection and the outcome following it. Do you know which part of you leads your reflections?

I used to conduct my own annual reflection with a critical eye. I looked at what I'd planned to do, what I didn't achieve, and what I needed to carry forward into the new year. I asked myself what I could do better, and my judger self confirmed that I needed to strive more and work harder.

I also spent time comparing myself to others. While it felt like reflection, it was really an act of futility and frustration. I thought comparing myself to the successes of others, their career advancement, their childrearing experiences, the trips they took, would drive me to pursue greater success. Remember how the comparison thief steals your joy? Comparing myself to others didn't drive me. It made me feel "less than." It made me feel like sh*t.

You might find when you reflect that you do the same thing. You may reflect with judgment or through comparison. It isn't surprising. We were taught to evaluate performance this way: focus on what needs improvement; aspire to be like those you admire; pursue leadership, advancement, and life by the metrics set out by your parents, your peers, and by society at large.

The thing is, the model is flawed. Can you improve? Of course!

Does it serve you to focus on what's wrong? Does it serve you to pay attention to how you don't measure up? Is this the way we're supposed to live our lives? By comparison?

And all the ways we didn't succeed?

Just writing it out now feels exhausting.

I was exhausted, but I didn't know there was a different way to be. I believed that if reflecting was a best practice, that was the way to do it. I didn't realize I had a choice.

Here is one of the most fascinating observations I've made as a workshop facilitator: When participants complete a practice session, I ask them to start by identifying what they felt they did well. Most people respond first with what they didn't do well, followed by what they want to do differently. So, I ask them again: "What did you do well?"

Often, they answer, "I don't know what I did well." It's clear that most of us are hardwired to focus on what's wrong.

Perhaps you were also taught not to boast. If you talk about yourself and what you did well, you're "bragging." I see people in workshop after workshop hold this limiting belief like a badge of honor. They believe that if they say what they did well, people will see them as overconfident or arrogant. This makes it hard to reflect on what they did well.

But isn't that where joy lives? Doesn't it feel markedly better to celebrate what went well? To focus on what was awesome?

If you took a moment right now to look back at all the work you've done so far, how would it feel to celebrate how far you've come? What would your heart want to celebrate?

For me, in discovering how I reflect is a choice, what could I change?

I started exploring cherishing moments. When I caught myself in a negative spiral during reflection, I'd ask myself questions like:

"What do I want to cherish today?"
"What do I want to celebrate?"
"What strength did I bring to my work today?"
"What did I learn today?"

Using these questions and inviting myself to cherish the moments transformed my whole reflection process. It quieted the IBSC and invited my heart to dance with me in my daily reflective practice. I leaned into my strengths, embraced opportunities to grow, and felt a whole lot happier too.

How could cherishing moments help you transform your reflective practice?

Trust the Universe

So far, we've explored the three types of trust I explore with my clients in my coaching practice: Trust in self, trust in others, and trust in the process.

One area of trust I don't talk too much about in my coaching work is trust in the universe. Yet, when I'm living by heart, I hear messages from the universe all the time. I know the messages have always been there, but when I lived by my warrior self, I couldn't hear them.

Do you trust in the universe? Ask yourself whether you believe the universe is with you and has your back. Notice if you feel any resistance or judgment. If this is the first time you've thought about your connection to the universe, you may feel some resistance or even feel judgment toward me. That's okay too. Your judger self might wonder, *What the heck is she talking about, hearing messages from the universe?* If that's the case, I invite you to choose whether to read this section or skip ahead. You always have a choice.

If you're unsure, you may want to take a moment to put your hand on your heart. Close your eyes if you wish and take a few deep breaths. What does your heart say? Perhaps she invites you to come to this section unattached and open. You can read it and then choose to do some work, or let it go.

Or you may have done work yourself in exploring your connection to the universe and you come to this chapter without any judgment or hesitation. All answers are the right one for you in this moment. If you're coming along, let's step into the learning together.

In my experience, hearing messages from the universe and trusting them are two different things. While I started hearing the messages at the beginning of my heart-led journey, it's taken me much longer to trust those messages.

I once asked Jason whether he trusted in the universe. He pondered the question for a moment and then said yes. Once he reached his conclusion, he was very certain. I admired that certainty. What prevented me from having that same certainty? *Hello, Comparison self.*

I've struggled believing things that seem too simple to believe. Doubt creeps in when something seems too easy. What is it about my ego that craves complexity? Why do I want to make things more difficult than they need to be? This is where my daily work on myself, my awareness, and trust all intersect.

When I check in with my heart, I do believe and trust in the universe. I see evidence of the magic of the universe every day, when I take time to notice it. There is a connectedness between me and all living things. There is a shared energy that moves between us, within us, and around us. I must slow down, breathe, and allow myself to witness the magic. It is everywhere. It is in all things. And it is within each of us.

When I let the magic in, my heart dances and twirls. She spins and delights. There is joy and peace. There is a great sense of calm. There is a knowing that all is well in the world. That the worries of the day are small in comparison to the greatness of the universe. The goodness in all things.

When I sit in wholeness, I am enough. I am overflowing with an abundance that eliminates all worry, all fear, and just rests— rests in the knowingness of it; rests without striving or battling or climbing. It is all as it should be in this very moment, and that brings peace.

Alternatively, when I am wound up with worry, I prevent the universe from working its magic. My IBSC loves it when I start worrying, and they host a dance party when I disconnect from the magic of the universe. I feel alone, isolated, and completely unworthy. Any challenge looks like a giant mountain I can't climb or a 5,000-piece puzzle that's missing all its pieces.

When I release from the worry, thank my IBSC for their concern, shut down the dance party and send them on their merry way, I see that the challenge isn't insurmountable. My heart helps me connect to the universe. I trust that the puzzle pieces will appear when they are ready to . . . and slowly those pieces start to appear.

Just because I know that I'm connected to the universe doesn't mean I always feel connected or receive the messages the universe sends me. Having a daily trust practice helps me connect to the universe and its magic. My daily practice reminds me that the worries, fears, and lack of worthiness I feel are all in my mind and within my control. It reminds me to slow down and really listen because the messages from the universe are waiting there for me to receive them.

Through a daily practice, I've learned how to connect with the universe. I've learned how to pause, how to connect with nature to feel the incredible vibration that travels through the earth into my feet. That same vibration travels through the trees and into my hands when I touch them. It travels on the wind and in the sunlight. Energetically, we are all connected and one with the universe. I am always connected to it. The daily practice brings me into the present moment so I can see it, feel it, and hear it.

I invite you to explore what activities connect you to the energy and magic of the universe. Try earthing, or walking barefoot in the grass, to connect and ground with the Earth's vibration. Forest bathing or simply going to a local park and touching trees can connect you to the wisdom and energy of the trees around you. Spending time in nature, in the sunlight, paying attention to the wind, or being near a body of water are all ways to connect with the energy of the universe. Take note of the activities that work best for you.

TREE MAGIC IN WINTER

As you read the story that follows, pay attention to your heart and ask what you feel curious about when you reach the story's end.

It was January 2017, and Toronto was deep in its weary winter weather. My mood reflected the grayness of the sky. I was cold, tired, and miserable as I trudged along the slush-filled street. My boots felt chilly against my scratchy wool socks, and I wondered whether the socks were damp from the watery mess on the sidewalk.

Just then, a car drove by too close to the curb and I was drenched head to toe with slush and salt. *Great. Just what I need on this dismal day.*

I glanced across the street and noticed a tree in the park. Despite the sunless, dreary day, the tree appeared to glimmer in the light. I felt a sudden pull toward it.

That's nuts, my judger self said with a scoff. *Just keep on walking.*

But I couldn't. I waited at the curb, fully prepared to be soaked again by an approaching car, to cross the road to the park.

You can't, Judger self cried out at me. *People will see you.*

I paused for a moment. *She's right. What will people think?*

Who is watching you? my heart asked. *No one, love. This is a gift for you alone.*

The traffic on the street cleared as if to offer me a path directly to the tree. This majestic tree with its barren branches. It looked so alive, but I couldn't understand how. It literally glittered before me, and it seemed to be breathing as I walked closer.

I felt myself glancing around, second-guessing myself. *Should I really do this?*

But the energy pulling me toward this tree was so strong I couldn't ignore it. My fingertips felt tingly, ignited by the energy from the tree. I felt a deep wanting, a craving to connect with this life force that shone out like a beacon in the darkness. The tree called to me, asking me to come closer, pulling me into her embrace.

Yes, said my heart. *Yes.*

As I neared the tree, I quickly pulled off my gloves, my hands feeling the bite in the cold air as the wind swept against them. I shoved my gloves in my pocket so my hands would be free of any barriers.

People are watching you, my judger self jeered, her warning ominous. My heart skipped a beat as I glanced around again. And suddenly I felt the warmth of the universe course through my veins and set my skin ablaze.

I care not. And I wrapped my arms around the tree.

My fingers spread wide across her bark. I could feel the texture of the ridges of years, decades, a century of history flowing through me. I felt the love emanating from this tree. I thought how magical it was that I assumed trees lay dormant in winter, and yet here was this glorious tree lighting up the park. Lighting up the neighborhood. Lighting up the world.

I stood there, hugging the tree, and felt a sense of healing wash over me. The dark, dreary misery I'd felt before I'd entered the park vanished, replaced with joy, and love, and awe for the beauty of nature. For the beauty of the universe. And I felt one with it.

I don't know how long I stood there holding that tree in the middle of a large, exposed park on a busy downtown street in Toronto. As I held her, I could not sense time or anything beyond the embrace.

When I finally released the tree, I spent a few moments giving thanks. I thanked the tree for her generous gift. I thanked Mother Earth for sharing the tree with me. I thanked the universe for this magical exchange. I thanked my heart for encouraging me to cross the street and receive this gift, right when I needed it. I even thanked my judger self for stepping out of the way for a moment so I could enjoy it fully.

Humph, she said. *You still looked stupid hugging that tree.*

I knew that while the struggle between head and heart continued, I'd listened to my heart and received exactly what I needed. I could choose to listen to her and be rewarded. That moment, that tree, the energy, listening to my heart, and the messages from the universe changed me that day. For the better.

What did you notice as you read that story? Were you paying attention to your heart? Or did your judger self take over? What can you take from this story to apply to your own trust practice?

How could stepping outside and connecting with nature support you? Could it help you build trust in yourself, others, the process, and the universe?

Give yourself space to reflect on the magic, energy, and power of the universe. If you can, step outside now and reflect in the fresh air. Notice the difference in your reflection when you connect with nature. What changes?

Trust as a Practice

Reflect on the tools you've gathered so far from this book and any tools you came with before you started reading it.

Do you need more tools or different tools to practice building trust? Or can you trust yourself that through the journey so far you have all the tools you need? If you hear an answer from your judger self or another member of your IBSC, or feel a sense of resistance, you can trust that this information is guiding you where to start your inner work.

If you started reading the Trust section of this book first, I encourage you to go back to the "As a Practice" sections in Healing, Empathy, Awareness, and Resilience where you'll find the many tools we've covered along the way.

Or you may hear your heart say, *Trust, love. You already have everything you need.*

There are no new tools to add here, just an opportunity to check in and ask yourself questions about trust. In this section I covered trust in self, trust in others, and trust in the process. I also talked about cherishing moments and trusting the universe. You can build your daily trust practice with the three simple questions we started with:

- Do I trust myself?
- Do I trust others?
- Do I trust the process?

As your practice evolves, you can check in on your progress through a daily reflective practice with additional questions like:

Trust in Self

- How did I trust myself today?
- Where did I doubt myself today?
- How can I trust myself more?

Trust in Others

- How did I demonstrate trust in others today?
- Where did I lack trust or feel resistance to trusting someone else today?
- What can I do to trust others more tomorrow?

Trust the Process

- How did I trust the process today?
- Where am I still trying to control the process?
- Where do I feel impatient or resistant to the process?
- What can I let go of?

Building your trust in yourself, in others, and in the process takes time. You can't rush trust, even if you want to. Believe me, I've tried!

As you challenge the stories that keep getting in your way, as you practice listening to your heart, as you reflect on where you can focus your attention to stretch, grow, and get a little uncomfortable, your trust in yourself will grow.

As you build your empathy, love, and compassion for others, as you practice believing that others are doing the best they can where they're at in the moment, as you let go of control and release from the hold of your ego, your trust in others will grow.

As you increase your own self-awareness, set intentions instead of goals, observe your patterns, track the changes that occur over time, and cherish the moments along the way, your trust in the process will grow.

I am forever a work in progress. You are too.

It isn't about the destination—it's about the journey.

That's what living by heart is.

Compassionate
WARRIOR

What Is a Compassionate Warrior?

When one part of you dominates the rest of you, you live out of balance. When your warrior dominates, you see the world as a battle and every interaction as a fight to win. The warrior can lead, succeed, and be rewarded, but she can also intimidate others and drive people away from you.

When your heart dominates, you see the world as love, sunshine and roses, and every interaction as an opportunity to connect and seek win-win outcomes. The heart can build deep connections with self and others, but she can also be too kind and fail to set boundaries or ask for what you need.

What's the best way to live in harmony with all parts of yourself? It's about bringing head and heart together.

By finding harmony within myself, I became the compassionate warrior. I invite you to bring the parts of yourself into harmony so you can stand strong as a compassionate warrior living by heart.

The Path to Compassionate Warrior

As children, we start out whole. We bring our whole selves to everything we do. There is no separation. No judgment or analysis. There is simply being—being who we are, thinking what we think, and most importantly, feeling what we feel just flows naturally from us.

Our feelings, our emotions, are pure. Unfiltered.

It is through the journey into adulthood, and the lessons we learn along the way, that we lose our wholeness. We start to edit. We revise. We delete the parts of us that don't "fit in."

I desperately wanted to be liked. I desperately wanted to be loved. I desperately wanted to "fit in." And in doing so, I lost large parts of myself.

My path is riddled with the greatness I discarded to be like everyone else. I feel a deep sadness when I write about it. To know that I had so much power, strength, and wholeness that I abandoned because I believed the lies I was told.

"You can't be strong and be liked."

"You have two ears and one mouth. Listen more than you talk."

"You want people to like you, don't you? Then don't be so forceful. Don't be so confident. Don't be so sure of yourself. People don't like that."

"Don't be bossy."

"Don't be pushy."

"Don't ask too many questions."

As I recall these messages, I hear myself thinking, *Oh my god! No wonder I morphed into a much-dimmed version of myself.*

The challenge for me was that my warrior spirit was still so strong, even with all these messages and trying so hard to fit in. My warrior spirit couldn't be fully contained. She tended to surface, sometimes angrily, when I was hurt, embarrassed, ashamed. She would leap out of her cage, breaking through the padlock, and rage about while trampling over everything and everyone in her path.

My warrior spirit wanted to protect me. Defend my honor and hurt anyone who hurt me. She was fierce and unapologetic. But when the dust settled, I was left to clean up the mess she'd made. And usually the pain was deeper, not better. Because now I had hurt others the same way I was hurting. I can see the patterns so clearly now. With my warrior spirit trapped in a cage, she only saw the light of day when things were bad.

Today, I am proud; I'm not worried talking about her. I'm not ashamed of my warrior spirit. I don't see her as a negative aspect of myself the way I used to. I embrace her power, and I channel it instead of being overtaken by it.

The other side of me is my compassionate side, the loving side that wants to ensure others never feel pain. The me who wants to take care of everyone, to forgive everything, and to live in peace and harmony with the universe.

During my life, I received concerning messages about this side of myself too.

"Nice girls finish last."

"Being nice won't get you ahead."

"If you are seen as nice, you won't be seen as capable."

"Nice girls marry well."

"Nice girls become great mothers."

"Be nice."

"Share."

"Let them go first."

So many mixed messages. Is it any wonder we can't figure out how to be our true selves? We receive so many messages telling us not to.

I won't let any of the parts of me go, even if I'm told to restrict or change them. All parts of me are worthy and are loved.

I've evolved from Warrior Goddess at the start of my journey, to Compassionate Goddess in the early years of reconnecting with my heart, to the Compassionate Warrior who brings the best of my head and my heart to how I lead and how I live.

I bring truth, love, peace, and fierceness to my work, my play, my life—everyday. This is who I am. I am a compassionate warrior.

Compassionate Warrior as a Practice

At the start of this book, I talked about building a daily practice for living by heart. Today, living as a compassionate warrior, I use many of the practices outlined in the HEART framework. I encourage you to take the practices from each section of this book that work best for you to create your own daily practice.

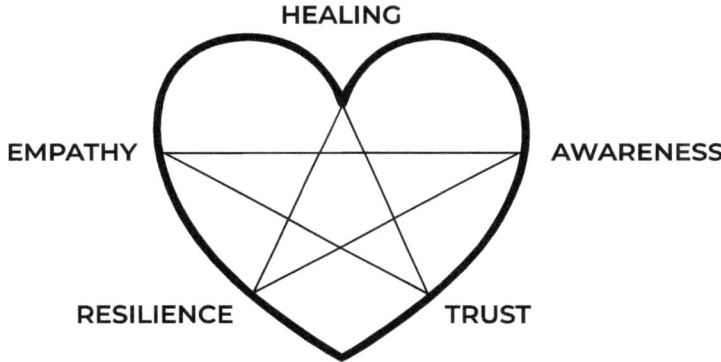

- Check in on the parts of yourself to see if you need more healing, empathy, awareness, resilience, or trust.

- Take time at the start of your day to set your intentions for how you want to be a compassionate warrior today.

- Reflect throughout the day and give yourself space for rest and renewal.

- Look back on your day to see what you learned, what you want to celebrate, and what, if anything, you might do differently tomorrow.

Bringing your head and heart together is a daily practice too. You may want to ask yourself questions like:

"What does my head say?"
"What does my heart say?"
"What part of me is needed in this situation?"

"What is within my control or influence?" If the answer is nothing, ask yourself: "How do I want to show up in this situation?"

If you feel like your heart needs a little more attention, ask:
"How will I love myself today?"
"What am I doing to love myself today?"

Before I started writing this book, I asked myself: "How will I love myself today?"

My heart answered. She said, *Write a book about Living by HEART as a love letter to yourself.*

So, I did.

As much as my warrior tried to fight it, and the IBSC told me not to risk it, I know that each page in this book was written as a loving act of service to me, to better knowing and loving myself, and in celebration of Living by HEART.

I hope you've enjoyed the journey. I hope you love yourself now more than you did before and, through your own practice, discover the magic of Living by HEART.

CALL TO ACTION

It's been a joy to walk with you on this journey to living by HEART!

Knowing that living by HEART is practice, and not a destination, let's stay connected.

Use the QR code below to visit livingbyheart.ca

Check out the Living by HEART website to share this book with others, leave a review, or to connect with me to explore coaching, workshops, or for a keynote at your next event.

Join the Living by HEART email list for updates, tools, and future books in the Living by HEART series.

ACKNOWLEDGMENTS

I dedicate this book in memory of my parents, who loved me, challenged me, and encouraged me. Mom, you taught me to believe in myself and supported me when I didn't. You also gave me boundaries and helped me learn to set my own. "No b*tching, no whining, and no complaining." Dad, you taught me to debate and challenge the status quo. You also taught me to have fun, take risks, and not take myself so seriously. I love and miss you both endlessly.

There are many places in my life that influenced me, but two stand out that I am so grateful for. Camp Oconto, the summer camp that for ten summers provided me a safe place to be my whole self and be surrounded and inspired by young women who lived wholeheartedly. Albert College, after years of struggling to connect in school, your hallowed halls provided me with the space to grow, learn, and embrace the musical side of myself unapologetically. My time here set me on a new course that would guide me toward the Compassionate Warrior I am today.

To the many friends who responded to my early writings and "Living by Heart" videos on Facebook, who connected with my stories, and encouraged me to write a book. I love you. I see you. I appreciate you.

Thank you to the WAVE Mastermind and the inspiring women entrepreneurs who supported and cheered me on during the writing and editing of this book. Your encouragement helped me through the tough moments so I could get across the finish line.

I'm grateful to the Adler Faculty of Professional Coaching where I learned the science and art of professional coaching and discovered an incredible coaching community. Thank you to my fellow coaches, my mentors, and the faculty—especially Brian, Anne, Fran, and Adria.

Special thanks to my editors, Amber and Christine, for your wisdom helping me tell my stories powerfully, assisting me in clarifying and adapting my message, and for honoring my voice.

I'm thankful for the expertise of my publisher, Sabrina at fEM-POWER Publications, for helping me birth this book and bring my dream into reality.

To all the women who attended a Roots and Wings Retreat or Women.Lead.Now. (WLN) Leadership masterclass, thank you for showing up with curiosity, openness, vulnerability, and courage. To the three women coaches, Corry, Stephanie, and Alicia, who collaborated to bring our visions to life—thank you for letting me learn how to trust others on our journey together and for inspiring my growth. A special thank you to Alicia, the cocreator of WLN and my business partner who patiently supported me as we learned to build incredible programs together.

Thank you to my dear friends Heather, Christine, and Rebecca, who have walked beside me as I traveled on my living by heart journey. Your support, encouragement, and love mean more to me than I can ever express. Thank you for believing in me writing this book.

To my sister, Catherine, thank you for walking beside me through the grief of losing Mom and Dad. I'm so grateful for you and for the relationship we've built together that's only grown stronger through our loss. Thank you for making me laugh, keeping the memories alive, and reminding me that we're both worthy.

To my three intelligent, loving sons, thank you for teaching me more than I ever imagined I'd learn. Thank you for your support and encouragement writing this book, for reminding me "Peaches, Mommy," and for inspiring me to live by heart always.

With love and immense gratitude for my rock-star husband, Jason. You always loved me and all my wacky parts and stood by me while I learned to love myself. Finding the Compassionate Warrior within me and writing this book to share the journey wouldn't have been possible without your unwavering support and belief in me. I love you.

RESOURCES
(in order of mention)

For more information on Dr. Richard C. Schwartz and Internal Family Systems, visit https://en.wikipedia.org/wiki/Internal_Family_Systems_Model

"This Is the Beginning," track 1 on BOY *Mutual Friends*, Grönland Records, 2011.

Whitworth, Laura, Karen Kimsey-House, Henry Kimsey-House, Phillip Sandahl. 2nd ed. 2007. *Co-Active Coaching: New Skills for Coaching People Toward Success in Work and Life*. UNKNO.

Enns, Adrienne. *Seeds of Intention: Daily Intentions for Living on Purpose*. Oracle cards. https://mayyouknowjoy.com/product/seeds-of-intention-cards/

"Brené Brown on Empathy." Brené Brown. Production and Editing: Al Francis-Sears and Abi Stephenson. Posted December 10, 2013, by RSA, YouTube. https://youtu.be/1Evwgu-369Jw?si=8wP_Uweg0sDWZ9Be

Hay, Louise. 1984. *You Can Heal Your Life*. Hay House.

Carroll, Willard, dir. *Playing by Heart*. 1998. Alliance Films.

For more information on Karpman's drama triangle, visit https://karpmandramatriangle.com/

Derrickson, Scott, dir. *Dr. Strange*. 2016. Marvel Studios.

"Uniform Grey," track 9 on Sarah Harmer *You Were Here*, Indie, 2000.

Brown, Brené. 2015. *Daring Greatly: How the Courage to Be Vulnerable Transforms the Way We Live, Love, Parent, and Lead*. Avery.

Led Zeppelin IV. Led Zeppelin. 1971. Atlantic Records.

"Fool in the Rain," track 3 on Led Zeppelin *In Through the Out Door*, Swan Song Records, 1979.

"Day 1 Simple Somatic Yoga, Connect Feet & Legs to Pelvis," Megan MacCarthy. Posted January 12, 2024. YouTube. https://www.youtube.com/live/cnyN-JcYkPQ?si=9Jc8vGrgjU7Udzpe

fEMPOWER
P U B L I C A T I O N S

At fEMPOWER, we help thought leaders and creative entrepreneurs capture their vision in the form of nonfiction books, journals, workbooks, affirmation cards, and personal growth products.

Our mission is to help our authors grow and scale a platform far beyond the book, protect their soul's work, and turn their message into a legacy!

www.fempower.pub
@fempower.pub

www.ingramcontent.com/pod-product-compliance
Lightning Source LLC
Chambersburg PA
CBHW051304120626
46547CB00015B/2084